GOLDEN RULES OF
ECONOMIC GROWTH

Golden Rules of
Economic Growth

STUDIES OF EFFICIENT AND
OPTIMAL INVESTMENT

BY Edmund S. Phelps

Professor of Economics,
Wharton School,
University of Pennsylvania

NEW YORK

W·W·Norton & Company·Inc·

For Charlotte

Contents

Contents

Preface

The purpose of this book is the exposition, generalization, application, and extension of the concept of the Golden Rule path in certain models of economic growth. The meaning and conditions for existence of the Golden Rule path in aggregative models is thoroughly expounded. Next, certain analogues and true generalizations of the Golden Rule path are presented; these Quasi-Golden Rule paths and Generalized Golden Rule paths indicate that the fundamental notion of a "commanding" growth path—of a path which gives uniformly higher consumption through time than any other path parallel to it in some respect—is encountered even in models in which no pure and simple Golden Rule path exists. These concepts are then applied in analyses of "dynamically efficient" economic growth and analyses of "socially optimal" economic growth in the sense of Ramsey. The Golden Rule path is then derived and characterized in more sophisticated aggregative models. Finally, the Golden Rule concept is extended to kinds of investment other than tangible capital formation: there is a Golden Rule of Research, a Golden Rule of Education and even such a concept in the context of population control. The book concludes with an extensive bibliography on the Golden Rule of Accumulation.

A word on the intended audience and use of this volume: despite the wealth of equations here, this book does not require more than elementary algebra and calculus. Second, once the introductory essay has been understood, most of the eleven remaining essays can be read independently of one another.

I wrote this book over several years, but mainly during 1964–1965 and 1965–1966 when I was a member of the Cowles Foundation at Yale University. In writing these essays I was assisted by numerous people and organizations, to whom I am very grateful.

The efforts of Tjalling Koopmans of the Cowles Foundation are fundamental to the essay on dynamical efficiency. (Only his insistence that the conjecturor of a theorem deserves more than half the credit saved him from co-authorship of the original article on which the first part of this essay is based.) Further, his promotion of the Golden Rule concept in such far-flung places as the Vatican and the U.S.S.R. has given me much encouragement.

David Cass, also of the Cowles Foundation, played an equally important role in the second part of that essay. In addition, considerable credit for the essay on the Ramsey problem must go to him. Cass was a source of constant mathematical solace in the years 1964 and 1965.

It was Christian von Weizsäcker of Heidelberg University who suggested to me that the investment-equals-profits path is a suitable generalization of the Golden Rule path. His published works on the Golden Rule, the Ramsey problem, induced invention, and vintage models have been important to the advancement of this volume.

James Tobin of the Cowles Foundation played a role in the analysis of the Golden Rule in the essay on vintage models and elsewhere in this book through his published works.

The essay on induced invention in the present volume is based on a paper co-authored by Emmanuel Drandakis, also a former colleague, who was induced to help me on the present, related essay as well.

Richard Nelson co-authored the article on education and growth which is in part the basis for an essay here on the Golden Rule of Education. In addition, Oiko has not forgotten his help in proving the Golden Rule theorem in the generality with which it appeared in my first published article on this subject. (It would have been a pleasure to reprint this "Fable for Growthmen" in this volume were it not that publication-embodied technological progress has made that piece obsolete with respect to rigor and scope.)

Perhaps it will cover half my remaining debt of gratitude to thank all my former colleagues at the Cowles Foundation and in the Department of Economics at Yale University for their interest and assistance in my work over the past few years. Of course, none of these people should be held responsible for any errors or other shortcomings of this volume.

Turning to organizations, I am grateful to Yale University and to the Cowles Foundation for Economic Research at Yale University for supporting my work on this book during the years 1964, 1965, and 1966. The financial support at the Cowles Foundation came from the Ford Foundation grant to the Massachusetts Institute of Technology and Yale University for the study of future United States economic growth. The book was completed during a leave of absence from Yale University during which time I was supported by Yale and by a Faculty Research Grant from the Social Science Research Council.

Finally, I am grateful to the editor of the *American Economic Review* for permission to use (with some modification) in the first and fourth essays material from my article "Second Essay on the Golden Rule of Accumulation," Vol. 55, No. 4 (September 1965), and to the editors of the *Review of Economic Studies* for permission to reprint (without substantial alteration) my article "Models of Technical Progress and the Golden Rule of Research" in Vol. 33, No. 2 (April 1966).

I am grateful to my wife, Charlotte, to whom this book is dedicated, for her encouragement of this undertaking.

Introduction

Anyone suddenly confronted by twelve essays in mathematical economics with recondite titles deserves a brief description of the contents. Herewith a short guide to these essays and some of the connections between them.

Part 1 of the book is concerned with the Golden Rule of Accumulation, its generalizations and application, in the simplest aggregative models of tangible investment and growth. The first essay states the meaning of the Golden Rule path and shows the conditions for the existence of that path. This essay can be understood without previous knowledge of the subject.

The next essay strays somewhat from the straight and narrow Golden Rule path. It presents a survey of the various kinds of "neutrality" that technical progress can possess, their relationship to the various kinds of factor augmentation, and gives an interpretation of the case of general factor augmentation. This essay shows that one of the conditions for the existence of the Golden Rule path is not satisfied—evidence that more general concepts of a "Golden Rule" path are required.

The third essay studies analogues and true generalizations of the Golden Rule path. These Quasi-Golden Rule paths and Generalized Golden Rule paths have the same property as the Golden Rule path: they yield uniformly higher consumption than growth paths absolutely or logarithmically parallel to them in terms of some variable.

The Golden Rule path, its analogues and generalizations are used in the following essay to demonstrate the dynamical inefficiency of certain growth paths, even paths with a continuously nonnegative social rate of return to investment. The analysis of such inefficiency is one of the two applications of the Golden Rule notion.

The other application of the Golden Rule is in the analysis of the "Ramsey problem" of optimal saving in a growing economy. The last essay in Part 1 contains new and old material on the use of the Golden Rule path in the solution of the Ramsey problem and in studying the existence of optimal paths.

Part 2 contains analyses of the existence and characterization of the Golden Rule path in models that are, in some respects, more sophisticated than those previously considered. The first essay presents a model of growth in which there is a problem of "absorption" into effective use of new capital formation. It is shown that the presence of an "absorptive capacity" in this sense in no way precludes the existence of the Golden Rule path.

The next essay in this part of the book departs from the earlier postulate that technical progress is wholly "disembodied." Two kinds of "vintage" models are presented in which technical progress is "capital-embodied": one with *ex post* fixed coefficients, the other with *ex post* substitutability. It is shown that the Golden Rule path is characterized in the usual way in these models.

The last essay in this part is to some extent a bridge to Part 3. In this essay, as in much of Part 3, it is recognized that, to a considerable degree, technological advances are produced, not exogenous. In particular, it is postulated in this essay that, given total inventive effort, inventors can choose among relatively labor-augmenting inventions and relatively capital-augmenting inventions, subject to an "invention possibility frontier." This view gives rise to a new theory of distribution and new complications in the theory of growth. After a short exposition of this model, the Golden Rule path is derived from it.

Part 3 extends the Golden Rule notion to research, education, and population growth. In the first essay, on research, and in the second essay, on education, it is assumed that technical progress is purely labor augmenting. But though the matter of the factor-saving bias of technical progress is side-stepped, there remains the important question of how the *rate* of technical progress—or, more precisely, the rate of labor augmentation—depends upon the magnitude of current research effort and other variables. In the first essay, several models of technical progress are examined in which the level of technology depends upon the past history of research effort. From one of these models a Golden Rule of Research is derived. This Golden Rule path is characterized by the equality of the rate of return to research with the golden-age rate of growth.

The second essay turns, inevitably, to education. Without maintenance of educational attainments per head, it is likely that technical advances realized in new processes and products would fall behind the technological advances in blueprints. This essay, which builds admittedly upon a very partial view of the connection between education and growth, develops a Golden Rule of Education that is analogous to the Golden Rule of Accumulation. An upshot of these two essays is that, quite possibly, society can invest more than is efficient not just in tangible hardware but also in technology and human capital.

The following essay is concerned with the implications for tax rates of private saving behavior in an economy in which total investment is determined by fiscal instruments of public policy. There seem to be some normative implications for private thrift in this model.

The last essay pertains to population policy. It is a very slender contribution to an enormously intriguing and complex subject.

The book closes with a bibliography of some forty-five papers dealing at least in part with the Golden Rule of Accumulation. It is intended to be complete for the years 1961–1965, though there are probably a few omissions. It is hoped that this bibliography repairs to some extent the failure of the present book to study the Golden Rule path in models of multisector and of open economies. The reader is referred to papers by Gale, Hamada, Robinson, Samuelson, Solow, and others listed in the bibliography which treat the Golden Rule path in such models.

Part **1**

GENERALIZATIONS
AND
APPLICATIONS

The Meaning and
Existence of the
Golden Rule Path

Several years ago, I presented a result on maximal consumption in a golden age.[1,2] Similar results were discovered and published by Maurice Allais, Jacques Desrousseaux, Joan Robinson, Trevor Swan, and Christian von Weizsäcker.[3,4] The theorem that has emerged can be expressed as follows:

If, in a model possessing a continuum of logarithmically parallel golden-age growth paths, there exists a golden-age path on which the social rate of return to (tangible) investment equals the golden-age rate of growth, and hence in neoclassical models, the fraction of output invested equals the capital elasticity of output—or, in market terms, a golden-age path on which the competitive interest rate equals the growth rate and hence gross investment equals the gross competitive earnings of capital—then (on a standard concavity assumption) this golden-age path produces a path of

[1] E. S. Phelps, "The Golden Rule of Accumulation: A Fable for Growthmen," *American Economic Review*, Vol. 51 (September 1961), pp. 638–643.

[2] A golden-age path is a growth path on which literally every variable changes (if at all) at a constant proportionate rate. Various other properties of "balanced" or "semibalanced" growth follow from this definition, as will be seen below.

[3] M. Allais, "The Influence of the Capital-Output Ratio on Real National Income," *Econometrica*, Vol. 30 (October 1962), pp. 700–728; J. Desrousseaux, "Expansion stable et taux d'intérêt optimal," *Annales de Mines* (November 1961), pp. 31–46; J. Robinson, "A Neoclassical Theorem," *Review of Economic Studies*, Vol. 29 (June 1962), pp. 219–226; T. W. Swan, "Of Golden Ages and Production Functions" in K. Berrill, ed., *Economic Development with Special Reference to East Asia: Proceedings of a Conference Held by the International*

consumption that is uniformly higher than the consumption path associated with any other golden-age path. Conversely, in neoclassical models, a positive-investment golden-age path which gives uniformly higher consumption than any other golden-age path is characterized by equality of the rate of return to investment and the golden-age growth rate. Thus, in neoclassical models, a necessary and sufficient condition that a positive-investment golden-age path yield uniformly higher consumption than any other logarithmically parallel golden-age path is the equality of the rate of return and the golden-age growth rate or of the investment-output ratio with capital's competitive share. In non-neoclassical, fixed-coefficients models where there may be a range of indeterminacy in factor prices, the consumption-maximizing golden-age path is characterized by the technological possibility *of equality between the competitive interest rate and the golden-age growth rate.*

The policy of maintaining the economy on the consumption-maximizing golden-age path—by continuously equating tangible investment to the competitive earnings of capital—will be called the Golden Rule of Accumulation, as I dubbed it in my earlier paper.[5] The consumption-maximizing golden-age path will be

Economic Association (New York: St. Martin's Press, 1964), pp. 3–16; C. C. von Weizsäcker, *Wachstum, Zins und Optimale Investifionsquote* (Basel: Kyklos-Verlag, 1962).

[4] The following related results should also be mentioned. The existence of a state of maximum per capita consumption with a growing labor force in a fixed-coefficients technology is shown in T. N. Srinivasan, "Investment Criteria and the Choice of Techniques of Production," *Yale Economic Essays,* Vol. 2 (Spring 1962), pp. 59–115. The theorem for the Cobb-Douglas case is found in an unpublished paper by M. J. Beckmann, "Economic Growth and Wicksell's Cumulative Process," Cowles Foundation Discussion Paper 120 (June 1961), and for a variant of the Cobb-Douglas case by L. M. Koyck and Maria J. 't. Hooft-Welvaars, "Economic Growth, Marginal Productivity of Capital and the Rate of Interest" in F. H. Hahn and F. P. R. Brechling, eds., *The Theory of Interest Rates: Proceedings of a Conference Held by the International Economic Association* (New York: St. Martin's Press, 1965).

[5] Phelps, *op. cit.* It should be noted that the policy of equating investment to profits will produce the Golden Rule path only if the economy is initially on that golden-age path. The Golden Rule path is that *golden-age* path on which investment equals profits, not *any* path with that property.

called the Golden Rule path. This terminology, which is now widespread, stems from the somewhat jocular suggestion of my earlier paper, written in the form of a fable, that, on this golden-age path, each generation saves (for future generations) that fraction of income which it would have past generations save for it, subject to the constraint that all generations stretching infinitely far in the past and in the future save the same proportion of income.

The present essay is concerned with the derivation and conditions for the existence of the Golden Rule path in an aggregative model having a neoclassical production function and in an aggregative model having a simple fixed-coefficients (Harrod-Domar) production function. In both of these models it is postulated that ("disembodied") technical progress is purely labor augmenting. That technical progress must be labor augmenting for the existence of the Golden Rule path is shown in the concluding part of the essay.

THE GOLDEN RULE PATH IN TWO MODELS

In both the neoclassical and Harrod-Domar models to be discussed, aggregate output at time t, $Q(t)$, is given by a linear homogeneous function of capital, $K(t)$, labor force, $L(t)$, and time, t, of the following form:

$$Q(t) = F[K(t), e^{\lambda t}L(t)], \quad \lambda \geq 0 \qquad (1)$$

where

$$mQ(t) = F[mK(t), me^{\lambda t}L(t)] \quad \text{for any } m \geq 0.$$

Output here is to be interpreted as capacity output.

It is postulated in (1) that technical progress (if any) can be described as purely "labor augmenting"; i.e., time enters only in the second (labor) argument of the function, rather than in the more general, "factor augmenting" way $F[B(t)K(t), A(t)L(t)]$ or the perfectly general way $F[K(t), L(t); t]$. It is as if the passage of time "augments" the labor supply. The constant, λ, is said to be the rate of labor augmentation, and $e^{\lambda t}L(t)$ is called augmented labor. (The conditions on which technical progress can be described as purely labor augmenting will be discussed.)

Labor is supplied inelastically and the labor force grows exogenously at the constant exponential rate γ:

$$L(t) = L_0 e^{\gamma t}, \quad \gamma \geq 0, \quad \gamma + \lambda > 0. \qquad (2)$$

Hence augmented labor grows at a constant rate, $\gamma + \lambda$, which we postulate to be positive.[6]

Capital is subject to exponential decay at the rate δ, so that if $I(t)$ denotes the rate of gross investment and $\dot{K}(t) \equiv dK/dt$ the rate of net investment, we have[7]

$$I(t) = \dot{K}(t) + \delta K(t), \quad \delta \geq 0. \qquad (3)$$

Finally, consumption, $C(t)$, which must be nonnegative, is the difference between output and gross investment:

$$C(t) = Q(t) - I(t), \quad C(t) \geq 0 \text{ for all } t. \qquad (4)$$

This is maximum consumption, given output and investment; actual consumption as the theorist frequently defines it would be less than maximum consumption if society threw away some of its output. (The national income accountant would perhaps label such waste as investment so as to make actual consumption equal to uninvested output.) As mentioned earlier, $Q(t)$ is maximum (or capacity) output from given $K(t)$ and $e^{\lambda t}L(t)$. Hence $C(t)$ in (4) is maximum consumption at time t, given $K(t)$, $e^{\lambda t}L(t)$ and $\dot{K}(t)$.

The Neoclassical Case By the neoclassical case we mean that the production function has the following "neoclassical" properties: it is twice differentiable (hence smooth marginal products), strictly concave (diminishing marginal products), and it has

---

[6] In the present model, it is the rate of growth of augmented labor that must be constant, not both the rate of labor augmentation and the rate of labor growth.

[7] This assumption is made for simplicity. It would be sufficient to suppose that the depreciation of every capital good is a function only of its age. No harm would result, I believe, if, further, the depreciation function were dependent on the rate of interest.

Note that throughout this volume, a variable with a dot over it, for example, $\dot{K}$, denotes the absolute time rate of increase of the variable, i.e., the total derivative dX/dt.

everywhere positive first derivatives (marginal products). Hence

$$\frac{\partial F}{\partial K} > 0, \frac{\partial F}{\partial L} > 0;$$

$$\frac{\partial^2 F}{\partial K^2} < 0, \frac{\partial^2 F}{\partial L^2} < 0. \qquad (1a)$$

By virtue of constant returns to scale in *(1)* and the exponential growth of labor in *(2)* we may write

$$Q(t) = L_o e^{(\gamma+\lambda)t} F\left[\frac{K(t)}{L_o e^{(\gamma+\lambda)t}}, 1\right]. \qquad (5)$$

Hence, if we let $k(t)$ denote capital per unit augmented labor,

$$k(t) = \frac{K(t)}{L_o e^{(\gamma+\lambda)t}}, \qquad (6)$$

and if we define

$$f(k(t)) = F[k(t), 1], \qquad (7)$$

we can express the production function for all t as[8]

$$Q(t) = L_o e^{(\gamma+\lambda)t} f(k(t)) \qquad (8)$$

where

$$f'(k(t)) = F_k[k(t), 1] > 0$$

and

$$f''(k(t)) = F_{kk}[k(t), 1] < 0.$$

This shows output per augmented labor to be an increasing, strictly concave function of capital per augmented labor. The first derivative, $f'(k(t))$, is the derivative of output per augmented labor with respect to capital per augmented labor, and it equals the derivative of output with respect to capital or the marginal product of capital, $\partial F/\partial K$.[9]

---

[8] F_k and F_{kk} denote the first and second partial derivatives, $\partial F/\partial k$ and $\partial^2 F/\partial k^2$.

[9] This can be seen from the equalities

$$f'(k) = F_k(k, 1) = L\frac{\partial}{\partial K} F\left(\frac{K}{L}, 1\right) = \frac{\partial}{\partial K} LF\left(\frac{K}{L}, 1\right) = \frac{\partial}{\partial K} F(K, L).$$

A fundamental concept in the present model is the notion of a golden age.[10] A golden-age path is a growth path on which literally every variable changes over time (if at all) at a constant proportionate rate. It will be shown now that golden-age growth with positive investment occurs if and only if $k(t)$ is a sustainable positive constant, so that golden-age growth is equivalent to constancy of $k(t)$.

First it will be shown that if $k(t)$ is equal to any positive constant $k > 0$, then golden-age growth results, provided of course that k is not so large that the feasibility constraint $C(t) \geq 0$ is violated. (Of course, there is a different golden age for each k.)

Clearly, output will grow exponentially at the rate of growth of augmented labor or "natural" rate of growth, $g = \gamma + \lambda$,

$$Q(t) = L_o e^{gt} f(k) \tag{9}$$

as will the capital stock:

$$K(t) = L_o e^{gt} k. \tag{10}$$

Hence $\dot{K}(t) = gK(t)$ so that, using *(3)*, we find that investment will also grow at the natural rate:

$$I(t) = (g + \delta)K(t) = (g + \delta)k L_o e^{gt}. \tag{11}$$

Since investment and output will both grow at the rate g, so will consumption, by virtue of *(4)*:

$$C(t) = [f(k) - (g + \delta)k] L_o e^{gt}. \tag{12}$$

The (gross) investment-output ratio, s, will be constant:

$$s = \frac{I(t)}{Q(t)} = \frac{(g + \delta)k}{f(k)}. \tag{13}$$

So will the capital-output ratio, x, (and hence its reciprocal, the average product of capital):

$$x = \frac{K(t)}{Q(t)} = \frac{k}{f(k)}. \tag{14}$$

---

[10] So called by Joan Robinson because it is "a mythical state of affairs not likely to obtain in any actual economy." *The Accumulation of Capital* (Homewood, Illinois: Richard D. Irwin, Inc., 1956), p. 99.

So will the marginal product of capital:

$$\frac{\partial F}{\partial K} = f'(k). \qquad (15)$$

Hence, capital's competitive (relative) share, a, which is equal to the capital elasticity of output, will also be constant:

$$a = \frac{\partial F}{\partial K}\frac{K(t)}{Q(t)} = \frac{f'(k)k}{f(k)}. \qquad (16)$$

Of course, there are many other variables that could be considered: the marginal product of labor, output per unit labor, output per unit augmented labor, and so on; it is readily seen that each of these variables changes (if at all) at a constant rate. Hence, constancy of $k(t)$ implies golden-age growth.

Conversely, it will be shown that, in the present model, every positive-investment golden-age path implies some constant value of $k(t) > 0$. By definition, every variable changes at a constant proportionate rate in a golden age; hence, if investment is positive, investment and output must grow at the same proportionate rate, say h;

$$Q(t) = Q(0)e^{ht} \qquad (17)$$

$$I(t) = I(0)e^{ht}. \qquad (18)$$

Capital must also grow at some constant proportionate rate, say m:

$$K(t) = K(0)e^{mt} \quad \text{or} \quad \dot{K}(t) = mK(t). \qquad (19)$$

Therefore, from *(3)*,

$$I(t) = (m + \delta)K(t). \qquad (20)$$

Hence, because $I(t)$ grows at rate h, $K(t)$ must also grow at that rate, so that $m = h$. Therefore output and capital grow at the same rate. By virtue of constant returns to scale in production and the positivity of the marginal product of labor, then, capital and output must grow at the same rate as augmented labor; hence $h = \gamma + \lambda = g$. Thus we have seen the equivalence of golden-age growth and constancy of $k(t)$.

This analysis also shows that these golden-age growth paths are "logarithmically parallel."[11] In particular, consumption on any golden-age path grows at the natural rate, $\gamma + \lambda$, so that the consumption path corresponding to one golden age never crosses the consumption path corresponding to any other golden age. This means that there may exist one golden-age path that gives higher consumption for all time than all other golden-age paths. We wish now to characterize the consumption-maximizing golden-age path—or Golden Rule path, as it is called—in terms of $f'(k)$ and s, each of which is a constant in any golden age.

Let us assume initially that the golden-age path yielding maximal consumption, if such exists, is one on which k (and hence $K(t)$ and $I(t)$) is greater than zero. Assume, in other words, that if a maximum exists, it is an *interior* one rather than a corner maximum at $k = 0$. Then, on this consumption-maximizing or Golden Rule path, the derivative of $C(t)$ with respect to k in *(12)* must be zero:

$$\frac{\partial C(t)}{\partial k} = [f'(k) - (g + \delta)]L_o e^{gt} = 0. \qquad (21)$$

From this we obtain

$$f'(k) - \delta = g. \qquad (22)$$

This states that on the Golden Rule path, the "net" marginal product of capital, $f'(k) - \delta = (\partial F/\partial K) - \delta$, is equal to the golden-age growth rate.[12] The left-hand side of *(22)* can also be

[11] For example, $\log K(t)$ on one golden-age path differs by a constant from $\log K(t)$ on any other particular golden-age path. There is such logarithmic parallelism in terms of any other variable.

[12] A common-sense explanation of this result has been provided by R. M. Solow in his "Comment," *Review of Economic Studies*, Vol. 29 (June 1962), pp. 255–257. Imagine that capital initially (at time zero) is free but that we are constrained to invest so as to maintain a golden age once the initial capital stock has been chosen. Consider a small increase of initial capital, $\Delta K(0)$. The rules of the game require that we then increase the initial rate of investment by $\Delta I(0) = (g + \delta) \Delta K(0)$ to make capital grow at rate g. The increase of initial capital will increase initial output by $\Delta Q(0) = (\partial F/\partial K) \Delta K(0)$. Hence initial consumption will increase by $\Delta C(0) = \Delta Q(0) - \Delta I(0) = [(\partial F/\partial K) - (g + \delta)] \Delta K(0)$. As long as $\partial F/\partial K > g + \delta$ it pays to accept more initial capital. The consumption-maximizing golden-age path is reached when $K(0)$ has increased to the point where $(\partial F/\partial K) - (g + \delta) = 0$, which is *(22)*. The reader should not conclude

interpreted as the social rate of return to investment.[13]   Hence this result states that if there exists an interior consumption-maximizing golden-age path, it is that golden-age path on which the social rate of return to investment equals the golden-age growth rate.   This is one way (and perhaps the best way) to characterize the Golden Rule path in purely technological terms.[14]

The other technological characterization is obtained by multiplying both sides of *(22)* by the capital-output ratio and rearranging terms so as to obtain

$$\frac{f'(k)K(t)}{Q(t)} = (g + \delta)\,\frac{K(t)}{Q(t)} = \frac{I(t)}{Q(t)} \qquad (\mathit{23})$$

whence

$$s = \frac{f'(k)k}{f(k)}\,. \qquad (\mathit{24})$$

---

that if we require capital to grow at some other constant rate $h \neq g$, then there is a consumption-maximizing path on which $\partial F/\partial K = h + \delta$, for in the present model there exists no path on which both the marginal product of capital equals $h + \delta$ and capital grows at rate h, $h \neq g$. However there will exist paths on which capital grows at some *variable* rate equal to the net marginal product of capital in both the present model and a more general model; such paths can be regarded as a generalization of the Golden Rule path as a subsequent essay shows.

[13] In a discrete-time model, the one-period social rate or return in period t is defined as

$$-\frac{\partial C(t + 1)}{\partial C(t)} - 1,$$

consumption in all other periods held constant.   In a continuous-time model, there exists an analogous notion of the instantaneous social rate of return. For a discussion of the social rate of return, see R. M. Solow, *Capital Theory and the Rate of Return* (Amsterdam: North-Holland Publishing Company, 1963).   Estimates of the social rate of return to tangible investment in the United States by the present author offer some evidence that the rate of return in that country in the 1950's considerably exceeded the long-term U.S. rate of growth.   See E. S. Phelps, "The New View of Investment," *Quarterly Journal of Economics*, Vol. 76 (November 1962), pp. 548–67, and Edmund and Charlotte Phelps, "Factor-Price-Frontier Estimation of a 'Vintage' Production Model of the U.S. Non-Farm Business Sector," *Review of Economics and Statistics*, Vol. 48 (August 1966).

[14] In my first essay on the Golden Rule (*op. cit.*) I eschewed this characterization out of fear that the Golden Rule path would be confused with the von Neumann path that exists in a quite different kind of model.

This states that on the interior Golden Rule path the investment ratio is equal to the capital elasticity of output. This was the characterization of the Golden Rule path made by Swan and the present author.

Conditions *(22)* and *(24)* can be translated into market terms if the economy is purely competitive and free of externalities in production. On these assumptions, $f'(k)$ is the gross rental rate on capital and $f'(k) - \delta$ is the rate of interest. Then *(22)* implies that on the interior Golden Rule path the interest rate is equal to the natural growth rate. And *(24)* implies that the investment ratio equals capital's gross relative share, a, or that net investment equals net profits.

Equation *(22)* or *(24)* is a necessary condition that a golden-age path give uniformly higher consumption than all other golden-age paths. Our postulate of everywhere diminishing marginal productivity of capital, however, implies that $f(k)$ is strictly concave, i.e., $f''(k) < 0$ for all k, so that there is at most one path satisfying *(22)* and this path gives a maximum rather than a minimum. Hence *(22)* or *(24)* is a necessary and sufficient condition that a golden-age path be consumption maximizing.

It should be noted that if $\gamma + \lambda = 0$ (contrary to our assumption) then each of our golden age paths is a stationary state. In that case, the stationary state in which the net marginal product of capital equals zero, i.e., $f'(k) - \delta = 0$, is the Golden Rule path. (This state will exist if and only if $f'(\infty) < \delta$, which requires $\delta > 0$ if $f'(\infty) = 0$.) Undoubtedly, the classical economists were aware that this zero-interest Schumpeterian state yielded uniformly higher consumption than any other stationary state.

Let us now investigate the conditions for the existence of the Golden Rule path. For this purpose we show in Figure 1 a diagram first used in Golden Rule analysis by Ivor Pearce.[15] It shows the dependence of output per augmented labor, investment per augmented labor, and consumption per augmented labor upon capital per augmented labor in a golden age, as given by the consumption equation in *(12)*.

---

[15] I. F. Pearce, "The End of the Golden Age in Solovia," *American Economic Review*, Vol. 52 (December 1962), pp. 1088–1097.

In Figure 1 there does exist an interior maximum, namely at $k = \hat{k}$ where the slopes of the two curves are equal, i.e., where $f'(k) = g + \delta$. It is easy to see, however, by manipulation of the two curves, that there are two cases in which no such interior Golden Rule maximum exists.

FIGURE 1

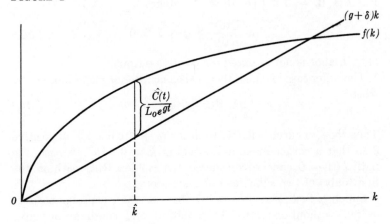

In one case, neither an interior nor a corner maximum exists. This is the case in which

$$\lim_{k \to \infty} f'(k) \geq g + \delta. \qquad (25)$$

Then the $f(k)$ curve is everywhere steeper than the $(g + \delta)k$ line so that the distance between them always increases with k. It should be noted, however, that this case can arise only if positive output can be produced without labor. This can be shown as follows. First, the inequality in (25) occurs if and only if

$$\lim_{k \to \infty} \frac{f(k)}{k} \geq g + \delta \qquad (26)$$

or, equivalently,

$$\lim_{k \to \infty} \frac{Q(0)}{K(0)} \geq g + \delta. \qquad (27)$$

Since

$$\frac{Q(0)}{K(0)} = F\left[1, \frac{L_o}{K(0)}\right], \tag{28}$$

we have

$$\lim_{K \to \infty} \frac{Q(0)}{K(0)} = F(1, 0). \tag{29}$$

But $F(1, 0) = 0$ if $F(K, 0) = 0$. Hence

$$\lim_{k \to \infty} \frac{Q(0)}{K(0)} \geq g + \delta > 0 \tag{30}$$

only if labor is not required for positive output.

The other case in which there exists no interior maximum occurs when

$$\lim_{k \to 0} f'(k) \leq g + \delta. \tag{31}$$

Then the $f(k)$ curve is flatter than the $(g + \delta)k$ line for all positive k so that a corner maximum exists at $k = 0$. In this case, the path $k(t) = 0$ can be considered the Golden Rule path in the first (only) of two subcases to be considered.

Suppose first that $f(0) > 0$; that is, there can be positive output without capital. Then output and consumption grow exponentially at the natural rate, as in any golden age:

$$Q(t) = C(t) = L_o e^{(\gamma + \lambda)t} f(0). \tag{32}$$

Hence the consumption path corresponding to $k = 0$ is parallel to all the other golden-age consumption paths. It is the maximal consumption path because of *(31)*, which implies that if a positive k were chosen, investment would have to be increased by more than would output increase. Hence the Golden Rule path is that path on which $k(t) = 0$ for all t.[16]

The other subcase is $f(0) = 0$. In this case the $f(k)$ curve lies uniformly below the $(g + \delta)k$ line (since both curves emanate from the origin and the $(g + \delta)k$ line is steeper for all $k > 0$). This implies that no feasible golden-age paths exist for which $k > 0$; $k(t) = k > 0$ implies negative consumption so that such paths are infeasible. Now $k = 0$ gives a "golden age" of a sort, for then output, consumption, investment, and capital are all

---

[16] On this path, investment equals profits, both being equal to zero. There could be equality of the interest rate and the natural growth rate.

zero (and hence change at constant rates); since this is the only golden-age path, it is the maximal golden-age path and hence could be regarded as the Golden Rule path. But this is probably unwise for two reasons: there is no family of golden-age paths of which one gives uniformly highest consumption. Second, part of the interest in Golden Rule paths pertains to the inefficiency of paths which keep $k(t)$ bounded above the Golden Rule level and such paths are infeasible in the subcase presently considered. Hence, I shall say that there exists no Golden Rule path in this case.

To summarize, the Golden Rule path necessarily exists in the present model if the marginal product of capital is less than $g + \delta$ for sufficiently large k and the marginal product of capital at $k = 0$ exceeds $g + \delta$ *or* capital is not required for positive output.

The Harrod-Domar Case No neoclassical assumptions such as those in *(1a)* are required for the existence of the Golden Rule path.[17] To illustrate this we now drop the assumption of twice differentiability, strict concavity and everywhere positive marginal products and specialize *(1)* to the Harrod-Domar production function:

$$Q(t) = \min [\alpha K(t), \beta e^{\lambda t} L(t)]. \qquad (1b)$$

We retain equations *(2)*, *(3)*, and *(4)*.

By virtue of *(2)* and the constant returns to scale postulated in *(1)* and exhibited in *(1b)*, we can write

$$Q(t) = L_o e^{(\gamma+\lambda)t} \min \left[\frac{\alpha K(t)}{L_o e^{(\gamma+\lambda)t}}, \beta \right] \qquad (33)$$

or

$$Q(t) = L_o e^{(\gamma+\lambda)t} f(k(t)) \qquad (34)$$

where

$$k(t) = \frac{K(t)}{L_o e^{(\gamma+\lambda)t}}$$

[17] The existence of the Golden Rule path in a complex fixed-coefficients technology with many capital goods was argued by J. Robinson in "A Neoclassical Theorem," *Review of Economic Studies*, Vol. 29 (June 1962), pp. 219–226. For a further discussion of the proposition see P. A. Samuelson, "Comment," *Review of Economic Studies*, Vol. 29 (June 1962), pp. 251–254.

and
$$f(k(t)) \ = \ \min [\alpha k(t), \beta].$$

It can be shown again that if $k(t)$ is equal to any positive constant $k > 0$ then, provided $C(t) \geq 0$, golden-age growth results. From *(34)* we see that output, capital, and investment will all grow at the constant rate $g = \gamma + \lambda$; hence, so will consumption. As before, $s = (g + \delta)k/f(k)$. If $\alpha k \leq \beta$, meaning that capital is fully employed, then $k/f(k) = K(t)/Q(t) = \alpha^{-1}$; if $\alpha k > \beta$, meaning that capital is in surplus, then $k/f(k) = K(t)/Q(t) = k\beta^{-1}$. The marginal product of capital, $f'(k)$, will be constant, either equal to α (if labor is in surplus) or zero (if capital is in surplus). The rate of interest will be $\alpha - \delta$ in the former case, $-\delta$ in the latter and indeterminate in the range between those two values if neither capital nor labor is in surplus.

Conversely, $k(t)$ is a positive constant in every positive-investment golden age. If investment (hence output and consumption) is growing at some constant rate, g, and capital is growing exponentially, then capital must also grow at rate g. Now if g were less than $\gamma + \lambda$, labor would become redundant (if it were not initially) and the unemployment ratio would grow nonexponentially, which contradicts the notion of a golden age; if g were greater than $\gamma + \lambda$, labor would eventually become scarce (if it were not initially) and growth of output at the rate g would then be impossible. Hence, in a golden age with positive investment, capital must grow at the rate $\gamma + \lambda$ so that $k(t)$ is constant. Therefore, golden-age growth with positive investment occurs if and only if $k(t)$ is a positive constant.

To investigate the Golden Rule path in this Harrod-Domar case we use Figure 2 which differs from Figure 1 only in that $f(k)$ is now $\min [\alpha k, \beta]$. Equation *(12)* remains valid so that we obtain

$$C(t) \ = \ \{\min [\alpha k, \beta] - (g + \delta)k\} L_o e^{gt}, \quad g = \gamma + \lambda. \quad (35)$$

The diagram displays an interior golden-age consumption maximum at $k = \hat{k} = \beta/\alpha$. This is the growth path on which both capital and labor are fully utilized. If the capital-augmented labor ratio were larger, capital would be in surplus; a smaller ratio would produce a surplus of labor. In the Harrod-Domar model, therefore, the Golden Rule path (if it exists) is that golden-age path on which there is full employment of both labor and capital.

FIGURE 2

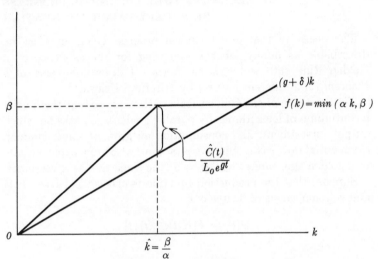

What of the usual characterization of the Golden Rule path in terms of the interest rate and capital's relative share? On the Golden Rule path, the investment ratio is $(g + \delta)/\alpha$ and the growth rate $\gamma + \lambda$. But relative shares and the interest rate are indeterminate: capital's share is between zero and one and the rate of interest is between zero and $\alpha - \delta$. Nevertheless this Golden Rule path is the only positive-investment golden-age path on which it is possible that capital's share equal the investment ratio and the interest rate equal the growth rate; in all other positive-investment golden ages, capital's share and the interest rate are determinate and fail to satisfy these equalities. Hence the characterization of the Golden Rule path in the Harrod-Domar model is not essentially different from that of the neoclassical model.

As in the neoclassical case, no Golden Rule path need exist. It is clear from the diagram that if $\alpha < g + \delta$ then there is no family of feasible golden-age paths—for then $k > 0$ will imply negative consumption—so that there is no Golden Rule path in that event.

THE NECESSITY THAT TECHNICAL PROGRESS BE PURELY LABOR AUGMENTING

The necessity that any technical progress going on must be describable as purely labor augmenting for the existence of a Golden Rule path will now be shown. I draw upon part of a theorem (of a different nature) by Hirofumi Uzawa.[18]

The existence of the Golden Rule path requires that there exist a continuum of logarithmically parallel golden-age paths on which output, investment, and consumption all grow at some common exponential rate, say g. Since capital must also grow exponentially in a golden age, capital will grow at the same rate as investment.

Suppose that the production function is neoclassical (see *(1a)*) and is homogenous of degree one:

$$Q(t) = F[K(t), L(t); t] \qquad (36)$$

or

$$\frac{Q(t)}{L(t)} = f(k(t); t) \qquad (37)$$

where

$$k(t) \equiv \frac{K(t)}{L(t)}.$$

Since the capital elasticity of output is less than unity, we can express output per head as a function of the capital-output ratio:

$$Q(t) = L(t)\varphi(x(t); t) \qquad (38)$$

where

$$k(t) = x(t) \frac{Q(t)}{L(t)}. \qquad (39)$$

Since output grows exponentially at rate g for every constant capital-output ratio, i.e., for every golden age, we have from *(38)*

$$L(t)\varphi(x(t), t) = L(t)A(t)\psi(x(t)) = H_o e^{gt}\psi(x(t)). \qquad (40)$$

[18] H. Uzawa, "Neutral Invention and the Stability of Growth Equilibrium," *Review of Economic Studies,* Vol. 28 (February 1961), pp. 117–124.

Hence

$$x(t) = \psi^{-1}\left(\frac{Q(t)}{L(t)A(t)}\right) \qquad (41)$$

and, from *(39)*,

$$\frac{k(t)}{A(t)} = \frac{Q(t)}{L(t)A(t)} \psi^{-1}\left(\frac{Q(t)}{L(t)A(t)}\right). \qquad (42)$$

Therefore $Q(t)/A(t)L(t)$ is some function of $k(t)/A(t)$, say

$$\frac{Q(t)}{L(t)A(t)} = m\left(\frac{K(t)}{L(t)A(t)}\right). \qquad (43)$$

Therefore, by constant returns to scale, the production function is of the form

$$Q(t) = M[K(t), A(t)L(t)] \qquad (44)$$

where $A(t)L(t) = H_o e^{gt}$. This shows that technical progress must, for the existence of the Golden Rule path, be describable as purely labor augmenting and that augmented labor must grow at a constant rate.[19] (It is not essential that $A(t)$ and $L(t)$ each grow exponentially. Of course, if labor grows exponentially, $A(t)$ must grow exponentially.)

The Robinson-Uzawa theorem[20] proves that technical progress can be described as purely labor augmenting if and only if progress is Harrod neutral everywhere (i.e., for all capital-labor ratios).[21] Hence we may say that a necessary condition for the existence of a continuum of logarithmically parallel golden-age paths, and hence for the existence of the Golden Rule path, is that technical progress be everywhere Harrod neutral.

Labor augmentation, of course, is a very restrictive type of technical progress. Nevertheless, the Golden Rule notion—the concept of a growth path which gives uniformly higher consumption than all other paths parallel to it in some respect—appears

---

[19] In the Cobb-Douglas case the function $K^\alpha(AL)^{1-\alpha}$ can be written $(BK)^\alpha L^{1-\alpha}$; what matters is whether the function *can* be written like *(44)*.

[20] Uzawa, *op. cit.*, and J. Robinson, "The Classification of Inventions," *Review of Economic Studies*, Vol. 5 (February 1938), pp. 139–142.

[21] Technical progress is said to be Harrod neutral if and only if capital's share (or the capital-output ratio) is constant over time when the interest rate or marginal product of capital is constant. A study of the various "neutralities" and kinds of factor augmentation is contained in the next essay.

even in models in which technical progress cannot be described as purely labor augmenting. These analogues and generalizations of the Golden Rule path, like the latter path itself, can be applied to the analysis of dynamically efficient growth paths.

Axioms for Factor-
Augmenting
Technical Progress

In much of economic growth theory it is postulated either that technical progress is purely labor augmenting or that progress is purely capital augmenting. There is increasing evidence, however, that if progress is factor augmenting at all, it is both labor and capital augmenting. Joan Robinson[1] and Hirofumi Uzawa[2] have given a necessary and sufficient condition (on the relationship over time between the average and marginal products of capital) for progress to be purely labor augmenting. There exists an analogous condition for progress to be purely capital augmenting. But the conditions under which progress is factor augmenting, meaning that progress is labor augmenting, capital augmenting, or both, has apparently not been explored. The purpose of this essay is to axiomatize the general case of factor-augmenting technical progress. The axiomatization produces interpretations of the rates of capital and labor augmentation.

Consider a production function which makes output, Q, a function of homogeneous capital, K, labor, L (both measured in physical units), and time, t:

$$Q = F(K, L; t). \qquad (1)$$

We suppose that there are constant returns to scale and that the function satisfies the usual neoclassical conditions of being twice

[1] J. Robinson, "The Classification of Inventions," *Review of Economic Studies*, Vol. 5 (February 1938), pp. 139–142.

[2] H. Uzawa, "Neutral Inventions and the Stability of Growth Equilibrium," *Review of Economic Studies*, Vol. 28 (February 1961), pp. 117–124.

differentiable with positive marginal products and diminishing marginal rate of substitution everywhere. Then

$$q = f(k, t) \qquad (2)$$

$$f_k(k, t) > 0 \qquad (3)$$

$$f_{kk}(k, t) < 0 \qquad (4)$$

where

$$q = Q/L \qquad (5)$$

$$k = K/L \qquad (6)$$

$$f(k, t) = F(k, 1; t) \qquad (7)$$

and

$$f_k = \partial f/\partial k, \quad f_{kk} = \partial^2 f/\partial k^2.$$

There is technical progress when $f_t > 0$.

Technical progress is said to be *Harrod neutral* at a particular capital-output ratio or its reciprocal, the average product of capital, if and only if, when the average product of capital is constant over time, the marginal product of capital (and hence capital's share) is likewise constant. (The capital-output ratio at which there is (local) Harrod neutrality may itself be changing over time.) Uzawa[3] has shown, on the above assumptions, that if and only if progress is Harrod neutral for *all* capital-output ratios, the production function can be written in the form

$$F(K, L; t) = G[K, A(t)L], \quad A(t) > 0 \qquad (8)$$

where $A(t)$ is a function only of time. Equation *(8)* defines *purely labor-augmenting progress*. So far as output and distributive shares are concerned, it is as if progress "augments" the labor input. The quantity $\dot{A}(t)/A(t)$ is said to be the (proportionate) rate of labor augmentation.

Similarly, John Fei and Gustav Ranis[4] have studied the counterpart for labor of Harrod neutrality. (They call it *U*-neutrality

[3] Uzawa, *op. cit.* Uzawa failed to emphasize, as I have tried to do in the text, that it is *global* Harrod neutrality—neutrality along all capital-labor paths—that is equivalent to pure labor augmentation.

[4] J. C. H. Fei and G. Ranis, "Innovational Intensity and Factor Bias in the Theory of Growth," *International Economic Review*, Vol. 6 (May 1965), pp. 182–198.

because they believe it to be of relevance for the analysis of underdeveloped economies.) We shall say that technical progress is *Fei-Ranis neutral* at a given labor-output ratio or its reciprocal, the average product of labor, if and only if, when the average product of labor is constant, the marginal product of labor (and hence distributive shares) is constant. By a proof similar to Uzawa's of the previous theorem, it can be shown that if and only if progress is Fei-Ranis neutral for all labor-output ratios, the production function can be written in the form

$$F(K, L; t) = G[B(t)K, L], \quad B(t) > 0, \quad (9)$$

where $B(t)$ is a function only of time. This defines *purely capital-augmenting progress*. $\dot{B}(t)/B(t)$ is the rate of capital augmentation. This special case of factor-augmenting progress, like the previous special case, is of importance.[5]

Progress is said to be *Hicks neutral* at a given capital-labor ratio if and only if, when the capital-labor ratio is constant, the average and marginal products of capital increase proportionally (so that distributive shares are constant). As is well-known, if and only if progress is Hicks neutral for all capital-labor ratios, the production function can be written

$$F(K, L; t) = G[A(t)K, A(t)L]$$
$$= A(t)G(K, L), \quad A(t) > 0. \quad (10)$$

The last equality follows from constant returns to scale. This might be called iso-factor–augmenting progress.

It may be remarked that these three neutralities coexist at a particular time and capital-labor ratio if and only if the elasticity of substitution is unitary at that k and t.[6] Hence, technical progress is simultaneously *everywhere* Harrod neutral (purely labor augmenting), *everywhere* Fei-Ranis neutral (purely capital augmenting) and *everywhere* Hicks neutral (iso-factor augmenting) if and only if $F(K, L; t)$ is Cobb-Douglas—where "everywhere" means "for all capital-labor ratios."

---

[5] In a one-good vintage model with *ex post* and *ex ante* substitutability alike, an "aggregate production function" representing aggregate output as a function of aggregate labor and "effective capital" exists if and only if all *capital-embodied* progress can be described as purely capital augmenting.

[6] See Fei and Ranis, *op. cit.*

Technical progress is said to be *factor augmenting* if and only if the production function can be put into the form

$$F(K, L; t) = G[B(t)K, A(t)L], \quad B(t) > 0, \quad A(t) > 0, \qquad (11)$$

where $B(t)$ and $A(t)$ are functions only of time. (If technical progress is to be nonnegative for all capital-labor ratios and all production functions satisfying *(2)*, *(3)*, and *(4)*, then both rates of factor augmentation must be nonnegative: $\dot{B}/B \geq 0$, $\dot{A}/A > 0$.)

We wish now to axiomatize *(11)* as previous writers have done for *(8)*, *(9)*, and *(10)*. Consider first the following proposition: given any initial capital-output ratio, there necessarily exists some positive function, say $P(t)$, such that when the average product of capital changes over time proportionally to $P(t)$, the marginal product of capital likewise changes proportionally to $P(t)$, so that distributive shares are constant. This says merely that there must exist some path of the capital-labor ratio (or equivalently some path of the capital-output ratio) which will preserve distributive shares in the face of technical progress. Without restrictions on the character of technical progress, the function $P(t)$ may differ for different initial capital-output ratios. (Of course, if $P(t)$ is constant for some initial capital-output ratio, we have Harrod neutrality for that ratio.)

Consider now the following restriction on the character of technical progress:

> Condition: *For all initial capital-output ratios, there exists a positive function $B(t)$, where $B(t)$ is a function only of time, such that when the average product of capital increases proportionally to $B(t)$, the marginal product likewise increases proportionally to $B(t)$, so that distributive shares are constant.*

This condition generalizes the concept of Harrod neutrality everywhere. It is clear that if $B(t)$ is constant, this is the condition for Harrod neutrality everywhere and hence for purely labor-augmenting progress. If $\dot{B} > 0$, and if the above condition happens to be satisfied when the average product of labor is constant, then we have Fei-Ranis neutrality everywhere and hence pure capital augmentation. If $\dot{B} > 0$ and the condition is satisfied by a constant capital-labor ratio, the progress is everywhere Hicks neutral and iso-factor augmenting. But these are merely special cases.

The following theorem will now be proved along the lines of Uzawa's proof of the aforementioned theorem on labor augmenting progress:

> Theorem: *Technical progress can be represented as factor augmenting, i.e., the relation (11) is satisfied, if and only if the above Condition is met.*

To express the theorem differently, if at time t the rate of change of the capital-output ratio necessary to keep shares constant is independent of the capital-output ratio, then (and only then) technical progress is factor augmenting at time t.

Proof: Sufficiency is proved first. By *(3)* and *(4)*, the production relation *(2)* may be transformed into one making output per head, q, a function of the capital-output ratio, denoted by x:

$$q = \varphi(x, t) \qquad (12)$$

or, without loss of generality,

$$q = \phi[B(t)x, t], \qquad (13)$$

where $B(t)$ is a function of t only and where x satisfies

$$k = xq. \qquad (14)$$

Differentiating *(13)* and *(14)* with respect to x, q, and k, we have

$$dq = \phi_1 B(t)\, dx, \qquad (15)$$

$$dk = x\, dq + q\, dx \qquad (16)$$

where ϕ_1 denotes the partial derivative of ϕ with respect to the first argument, $B(t)x$.

Solving *(15)* and *(16)* with respect to dq and dk, we obtain

$$\frac{\partial q}{\partial k} = \frac{\phi_1 B(t)}{\phi + B(t)x\phi_1}. \qquad (17)$$

Now if the previously stated Condition is satisfied, then there exists some function $B(t) > 0$, such that, for all x, $(\partial q/\partial k)B(t)^{-1}$ is constant when $B(t)x$ is constant. Then the right-hand side of

(18) below is independent of the second argument, t, being a function only of $B(t)x$:

$$\frac{\partial q}{\partial k} \frac{1}{B(t)} = \frac{\phi_1[B(t)x, t]}{\phi[B(t)x, t] + B(t)x\phi_1[B(t)x, t]}. \tag{18}$$

That is,

$$\frac{\phi_1[B(t), x]}{\phi[B(t)x, t] + B(t)x\phi_1[B(t)x, t]} = h[B(t)x], \tag{19}$$

where $h[B(t)x]$ is a function of $B(t)x$ only.

From *(19)* we have

$$\frac{\phi_1}{\phi} = \frac{h[B(t)x]}{1 - B(t)xh[B(t)x]}. \tag{20}$$

The relation *(20)* indicates that ϕ_1/ϕ is independent of the argument t; hence the function $\phi[B(t)x, t]$ is decomposable:

$$\phi[B(t)x, t] = A(t)\psi[B(t)x]. \tag{21}$$

From *(13)* and *(21)* we have

$$B(t)x = \psi^{-1}\left[\frac{q}{A(t)}\right], \tag{22}$$

where ψ^{-1} is the inverse function of ψ.

The relation *(22)* together with *(14)* imply

$$\frac{B(t)k}{A(t)} = \frac{q}{A(t)} \psi^{-1}\left[\frac{q}{A(t)}\right]. \tag{23}$$

Hence $q/A(t) = Q/A(t)L$ is some function of $B(t)k/A(t) = B(t)K/A(t)L$,

$$\frac{q}{A(t)} = g\left[\frac{B(t)k}{A(t)}\right] \tag{24}$$

or

$$Q = A(t)Lg\left[\frac{B(t)K}{A(t)L}\right]. \tag{25}$$

Therefore

$$Q = G[B(t)K, A(t)L] \tag{26}$$

where $G(K, L) = g(k)L$.

To prove necessity, let the relation *(11)* be satisfied. Then output per augmented labor is some function of the ratio of augmented capital to augmented labor, by virtue of constant returns to scale:

$$q = A(t)g\left[\frac{B(t)k}{A(t)}\right], \text{ say}. \qquad (27)$$

By virtue of *(3)* and *(4)*, the augmented capital-output ratio is a monotonically increasing function of the augmented-capital–augmented-labor ratio, so that we may write

$$q = A(t)\psi[B(t)x] \qquad (28)$$

for some $\psi[B(t)x]$. Hence

$$\frac{\phi_1}{\phi + B(t)x\phi_1} = \frac{\psi'[B(t)x]}{\psi[B(t)x] + B(t)x\psi'[B(t)x]}, \qquad (29)$$

which is independent of t, being a function only of $B(t)x$. Hence, from *(18)*, $(\partial q/\partial k)B(t)^{-1}$ is independent of t for constant $B(t)x$, i.e., for average product of capital increasing proportionally with $B(t)$. Hence, when $F(K, L; t)$ is of the form *(11)*, our Condition is satisfied. Q.E.D.

It should be remarked that our Condition could have been expressed in terms of the average and marginal products of labor. The condition would then be that, for every initial labor-output ratio, there exists a positive function $A(t)$ such that when the average product of labor increases proportionally with $A(t)$, the marginal product also increases in proportion to $A(t)$, so that distributive shares are constant. It can be proved analogously to the above proof that technical progress is describable as factor augmenting if and only if this latter condition is met. Therefore these two conditions are equivalent.

The "necessity" part of the theorem shows that the rate of capital augmentation can be interpreted as the rate of increase of the output-capital ratio when factor shares are constant; similarly, the rate of labor augmentation can be interpreted as the rate of increase of the output-labor ratio when shares are constant.

It is of interest to relate the *rate* of technical progress and various measures of the *bias* of technical progress to the (proportionate) rates of labor and capital augmentation, $\hat{A}$ and $\hat{B}$ respectively. The rate of technical progress, R, is defined by

$$R(k, t) = F_t/F. \qquad (30)$$

The measure of Hicksian bias, $\widetilde{B}$, used by Fei and Ranis, Peter Diamond,[7] and others, is the proportionate rate of increase of F_K/F_L for fixed capital-labor ratio. Hence

$$\widetilde{B}(k, t) = (F_{Kt}/F_K) - (F_{Lt}/F_L). \qquad (31)$$

Both R and $\widetilde{B}$ may be functions of k and t. At a given k, capital's competitive share will be increasing (decreasing) if $\widetilde{B} > 0$ (<0). Thus progress is, in the Hicksian sense, labor saving, neutral, or capital saving according as $\widetilde{B} > 0$, $\widetilde{B} = 0$, or $\widetilde{B} < 0$.

Further, we have

$$a(k, t) = F_K K/F = G_1 B(t)K/G \qquad (32)$$

$$\sigma(k, t) = F_K F_L/F F_{KL} = G_1 G_2/G G_{12} \qquad (33)$$

where $a(k, t)$ denotes the capital elasticity of output (capital's competitive share), $\sigma(k, t)$ the elasticity of substitution, and subscripts partial derivatives of the functions $F(K, L; t)$ and $G[B(t)K, A(t)L]$.

Differentiating $Q = G[B(t)K, A(t)L]$ partially with respect to time yields

$$R = a\hat{B} + (1 - a)\hat{A} \qquad (34)$$

where $\hat{X}$ denotes the proportionate rate of change of any variable $X(t)$ over time, i.e., $(dX/dt)/X$.

Using (32), and (33), and linear homogeneity of G, one can derive the following:

$$\frac{F_{Kt}}{F_K} = \hat{B} - \frac{1 - a}{\sigma} (\hat{B} - \hat{A}) \qquad (35)$$

$$\frac{F_{Lt}}{F_L} = \hat{A} + \frac{a}{\sigma} (\hat{B} - \hat{A}). \qquad (36)$$

Hence

$$\widetilde{B} = \frac{1 - \sigma}{\sigma} (\hat{A} - \hat{B}). \qquad (37)$$

Thus progress which is predominantly labor augmenting ($\hat{A} - \hat{B} > 0$) will be Hicks-labor saving ($\widetilde{B} > 0$), neutral, or capital saving according as the elasticity of substitution is less

[7] P. A. Diamond, "Disembodied Technical Change in a Two-Sector Model," *Review of Economic Studies*, Vol. 32 (April 1965), pp. 161–168.

than, equal to, or greater than one. Factor-augmenting progress is always Hicks neutral when $\sigma = 1$.

I shall define the Harrodian bias of technical progress, H, as the (proportionate) rate of growth of the marginal product of capital (equivalently, of capital's share) when the capital-output ratio is fixed. Then, as can be seen from Fei and Ranis,[8] H is related to R and $\widetilde{B}$ as follows:

$$H(k, t) = \left(\frac{\sigma - 1}{\sigma}\right) R + (1 - a)\widetilde{B}. \qquad (38)$$

Technical progress is Harrod neutral at given k and t, if $H = 0$. If $H > 0$, the marginal product of capital is rising for given capital-output ratio, so that capital's share is rising; such technical change will be called labor saving in Harrod's sense. Similarly, $H < 0$ indicates capital saving progress in Harrod's sense.

Finally, I define a measure of bias in the sense of Fei and Ranis. Let Z be the (proportionate) rate of increase of the marginal product of labor (equivalently, of labor's share) when the labor-output ratio is fixed. Then, as can be seen from Fei and Ranis,[9]

$$Z(k, t) = \frac{\sigma - 1}{\sigma} R - a\widetilde{B}. \qquad (39)$$

Progress is Fei-Ranis neutral if $Z = 0$. If $Z > 0$, labor's share is rising and so progress is Fei-Ranis labor using (or capital saving). If $Z < 0$, progress is Fei-Ranis labor saving.

Using the expressions for R and $\widetilde{B}$ in terms of $\hat{A}$ and $\hat{B}$ that appear in *(34)* and *(37)*, we find that

$$H = \frac{\sigma - 1}{\sigma} \hat{B} \qquad (40)$$

$$Z = \frac{\sigma - 1}{\sigma} \hat{A}. \qquad (41)$$

Hence, if technical progress is factor augmenting and if $\sigma \neq 1$, then Harrod neutrality requires zero capital augmentation while

[8] Fei and Ranis use D as a measure of Harrodian bias, where D is defined as the rate of increase of the capital-output ratio at a given marginal product of capital. From their equation (2.3), it can be seen that $D = \sigma H$, so that the two measures will have the same algebraic sign.

[9] Fei and Ranis use U, the rate of increase of the labor-output ratio for a fixed marginal product of labor. From their (4.3) we have $U = \sigma Z$.

Fei-Ranis neutrality requires zero labor augmentation. Suppose that, as is widely believed, $\sigma < 1$ in the relevant range, and suppose further that both rates of factor augmentation are positive (for which there is some evidence in studies that postulate factor augmentation). Then technical progress is capital saving in the sense of Harrod and it is labor saving in the sense of Fei and Ranis.

Let us adopt an aggregative model—with purely disembodied, factor-augmenting progress—of growth in the United States business sector over the past five or six decades. The special character of that growth allows us to compute the average rates of factor augmentation without knowledge of the elasticity of substitution. The previous theorem permits us to identify $\hat{B}$ as the rate of increase of the output-capital ratio, and $\hat{A}$ as the rate of increase of the output-labor ratio, when factor shares are constant. Since factor shares have shown little trend in the U.S. while the capital-output ratio has declined over the past fifty years at roughly 0.5 percent per annum and output per unit of labor has increased at roughly 2.5 percent per annum, we may conclude that, on average, $\hat{B} = 0.005$ and $\hat{A} = 0.025$. If these estimates are correct, progress has been predominantly labor augmenting, but not purely labor augmenting.

Unfortunately, it is not possible to read from the data the elasticity of substitution.[10] We require statistical technique (using time series exhibiting variability)—involving assumption of constant substitution elasticity or of some relationship between the elasticity and the ratio of augmented capital to augmented labor.

When such statistical analysis of production models has advanced considerably, we will be able to make some appraisal of the empirical *convenience* of the factor augmentation hypothesis. But we will never be able to refute it for it will always be possible to give a factor augmentation interpretation of any past growth path, even if the path of the substitution elasticity is prespecified. That is perhaps the charm of the hypothesis. But it may not be— undoubtedly, it is not—a correct hypothesis. The theorist is wise to use it sparingly, only for the sake of more general theorems which its use may suggest.

[10] We have only two independent equations—one for the growth of output and the other for the growth of one factor price (or share)—containing three unknowns, $\hat{A}$, $\hat{B}$, and σ.

Quasi- and Generalized Golden Rule Paths:

A Study of Commanding Growth Paths

The Golden Rule path is the golden-age growth path which gives higher consumption at every point in time than any other golden-age path. These other golden-age paths are all "parallel" to the Golden Rule path. The parallelism may be defined in terms of any of several variables. For example, since the capital-augmented labor ratio on any golden-age path is a constant (different for each golden age), there is a constant difference (positive or negative) between the capital-augmented labor ratio on the Golden Rule path and that on any other particular golden-age path; the two paths therefore are equidistant or "absolutely" parallel in terms of this ratio. All golden-age paths are parallel to the Golden Rule path in terms of the capital-output ratio and the rate of interest in precisely the same way. With respect to the capital stock, the parallelism is slightly different: on any particular golden-age path, the ratio of the capital stock to the Golden Rule capital stock is a constant. Equivalently, the difference between the logarithm of the capital stock on the golden age path and the logarithm of the Golden Rule capital stock is a constant. This may be called "relative" or "logarithmic" parallelism. (There is also such logarithmic parallelism in terms of the capital-output ratio and the rate of interest.)

Hence, the Golden Rule path is a growth path that gives uniformly higher consumption than any path that is parallel in one of the above respects. It is tempting to say that the Golden Rule path is a "dominating" path, that it "dominates" (with respect to consumption) all other parallel paths. But probably such use of the term "dominate" would be unfortunate.

I shall use the term "dominate" only in the following—I believe, customary—sense. A growth path is said to *dominate* another growth path if and only if both paths are feasible from the same initial conditions (capital good endowments) and if the former gives more consumption at least some of the time and never less consumption. Provided that consumption is the only desideratum and that more consumption is always preferred to less, any path which is dominated (in this sense) is dynamically inefficient (even if the statical efficiency conditions for maximum output are satisfied at every point in time) and therefore cannot be optimal.

It will be convenient expositionally, and it will help to reinforce an important distinction, to have another term to characterize a growth path which gives more consumption some of the time and never less consumption than another path, regardless of difference in initial state. I shall say that a growth path *commands* another path if, beginning at the present time and forever after, it gives higher consumption at least some of the time and never less consumption, *whether or not initial conditions are the same on the two paths*. The path giving the higher consumption (at least some of the time) will be said to be the *commanding* path. This property will be said to be the property of command.[1]

It is clear that command is a wider concept than dominance, since the former concept is not restricted to paths originating from the same initial state. Not every path which commands another path also dominates that path; only if the two paths start from the same initial state is the commanding path also a dominating path. On the other hand, every dominating path is a commanding path. Hence, of two paths one of which commands the other, the

---

[1] I have chosen this term only after much thought, research, and consultation. "Command" is exactly synonymous with "dominate" in the nontechnical sense of the latter term which corresponds to the technical use of that term. According to *Webster's New International Dictionary* (second edition), "to dominate" means "to have a commanding position over" (used transitively) or "to occupy a superior position" (used intransitively). "To command" means "to dominate in situation, as by height; also, to overlook" (used transitively) or "to dominate or overlook as from a superior position" (used intransitively).

commanding path is a dominating path if and only if the two paths start from the same initial state.

In these terms, the Golden Rule path is a commanding growth path: it commands all paths which are parallel to it in any of the aforementioned respects, i.e., it commands all other golden-age paths. It does not dominate these paths—any of them—because each of them starts with an initial capital stock different from the Golden Rule initial capital stock.[2] (However, some of these golden-age paths are dominated by certain *other* paths, paths which bear a close connection to the Golden Rule path, as Footnote 2 indicates.)

The immediate and ostensible purpose of this essay is to discover paths, other than the Golden Rule path, which command all paths parallel to them. Even in the Golden Rule model, in which pure labor augmentation and labor-force growth are exponential, it will be seen that the Golden Rule path is not the only path commanding all paths parallel (in some respect) to it. (But it appears that every such commanding path which is efficient, i.e., not dominated by another path, is asymptotic to the Golden Rule path.) The search for commanding paths is especially interesting in models not having those special features of exponential labor augmentation and labor-force growth, since, in such a model, no Golden Rule path exists (in the standard sense of a consumption-maximizing golden-age path).

Some of these commanding growth paths I call Quasi-Golden Rule paths and others Generalized Golden Rule paths. Any path which commands all paths parallel to it might well be called a Quasi-Golden Rule path since it is like the Golden Rule path in having this command property. But I elevate such a path to the status of a Generalized Golden Rule path if both of the following

[2] It is sometimes said, contrariwise, that any golden-age path which keeps the capital stock *in excess* of the Golden Rule capital stock is truly dominated by the Golden Rule path. What is *intended* by this statement, though it does not say it, is that such a golden-age path is dominated, for example, by a path which (necessarily) starts from the same initial (and excessive) capital stock and on which the "excess" capital is immediately consumed (or thrown away) and the Golden Rule path is followed thereafter. (Golden-age paths with always less capital then the Golden Rule path are not dominated because society cannot make up the initial "deficiency" of capital without giving up initial consumption.) Analysis of these topics is contained in the next essay.

conditions are satisfied. First, the path is a commanding path in a quite *general* (aggregative) model, i.e., a model in which there may be any number of primary inputs (land and labor of various varieties) and in which (exogenous) technical progress is arbitrary with respect to rate and factor-saving bias. Second, in the special case where the general model is equivalent to the Golden Rule model (with exponentially growing augmented labor), the commanding path must reduce to the pure and simple Golden Rule path for suitable initial conditions. (This requires that the kind of parallelism be similar in terms of some variable to the parallelism between the Golden Rule and golden-age paths.)

Why do I devote an essay to the study of commanding paths? The study of command in this essay serves as a prelude to the study of dominance, and hence of dynamical efficiency, contained in the next essay. I assign a separate essay to this study primarily for expositional convenience. In addition, the notion of a commanding path, like the Golden Rule notion, seems to possess interest or curiosity value independently of its applications to efficient and to optimal growth.

QUASI-GOLDEN RULE PATHS

It is postulated throughout this section that there is just one nonconstant primary resource, labor; it is a continuously differentiable function of time. The aggregate production function is posited to be homogeneous of degree one in capital and labor. (The existence and essential characterizations of the Quasi-Golden Rule paths in this section will continue to hold for production functions which are homogeneous of any positive degree.) The function is twice differentiable with everywhere positive marginal products and diminishing marginal productivity of capital and of labor. There is positive technical progress but the standard Golden Rule postulate that progress is purely labor augmenting and that augmented labor grows exponentially (so that there is a "natural" or golden-age growth rate) is abandoned. Hence the production function

$$Q = F(K, L; t)$$

satisfies the relations

$$F_K, F_L, F_t > 0,$$
$$F_{KK} < 0, F_{LL} < 0, \qquad (2)$$
$$F_K K + F_L L = Q.$$

In the early analysis, however, we place some restrictions on the factor-saving character of technical progress.

Pure Labor Augmentation As a first step, let us continue to suppose that technical progress is purely labor augmenting but let us relax the postulate that augmented labor grows at a constant exponential rate. Then our production function takes the form

$$Q = G(K, AL), \quad A > 0 \qquad (3)$$

where A is a function of time only—an increasing continuously differentiable function of time. It will be supposed that, for all t,

$$\frac{\dot{L}}{L} + \frac{\dot{A}}{A} > 0 \qquad (4)$$

where a variable with a dot over it denotes the absolute time rate of increase of the variable (its first total derivative with respect to time). The left-hand side of (4), the (proportionate) rate of growth of augmented labor, need not be constant.

We now develop an equation for consumption in terms of the ratio of capital to augmented labor, say k, and its absolute rate of change, $\dot{k}$. Taking depreciation to be zero, we have

$$C = G(K, AL) - \dot{K} \qquad (5)$$

or

$$C = \left[\frac{G(K, AL)}{AL} - \frac{\dot{K}}{AL} \right] AL. \qquad (5a)$$

The first term in the brackets, output per unit augmented labor, is a function of capital per unit augmented labor on our assumption of linear homogeneity:

$$\frac{G(K, AL)}{AL} = G\left(\frac{K}{AL}, 1\right) \equiv g(k), k \equiv \frac{K}{AL}. \qquad (6)$$

The derivative, $g'(k)$, is G_K, the marginal product of capital. Diminishing marginal productivity implies $g''(k) < 0$.

By differentiation of k with respect to time we obtain

$$\dot{k} = \frac{\dot{K}}{AL} - \left(\frac{\dot{L}}{L} + \frac{\dot{A}}{A}\right) k. \qquad (7)$$

This states that the absolute rate of increase of k is equal to the excess of investment per augmented labor over that amount necessary to keep k constant.

Substitution of *(6)* and *(7)* into *(5a)* yields

$$C = \left[g(k) - \left(\frac{\dot{L}}{L} + \frac{\dot{A}}{A}\right) k - \dot{k}\right] AL. \qquad (8)$$

The following propositions will now be shown. If there exists a path, say $\hat{k}(t)$, which commands all other paths absolutely parallel to it in terms of the capital-augmented labor ratio, then this path is uniquely characterized by equality between the marginal product of capital and the (proportionate) rate of growth of augmented labor:

$$g'(\hat{k}(t)) = \frac{\dot{L}(t)}{L(t)} + \frac{\dot{A}(t)}{A(t)}. \qquad (9)$$

Conversely, if there exists a path satisfying *(9)*, this path commands all others absolutely parallel to it in terms of the capital-augmented labor ratio. In other words, equality of the marginal product of capital and the rate of growth of augmented labor is a necessary and sufficient condition for a path to be a commanding path in the above sense. All this assumes that $\hat{k}(t) > 0$ for all t.[3]

Consider an arbitrary path $\bar{k}(t)$, feasible or not feasible. The paths absolutely parallel to it are defined by

$$k(t) = \bar{k}(t) + \delta \qquad (10)$$

where δ is a constant parameter, positive or negative.[4] Noting

[3] If $\hat{k}(t) = 0$ for some t, the equality sign in *(9)* is replaced by a less-than inequality sign for those values of t.

[4] Clearly, these parallel paths will be infeasible—i.e., require negative $k(t)$ or else investment in excess of output—for sufficiently large absolute values of δ. Also, $\bar{k}(t)$ itself may be infeasible.

that $\dot{k}(t) = \dot{\bar{k}}(t)$ for all t, we find, from *(8)*, that the consumption path corresponding to any given δ—positive, zero, or negative—is given by

$$C(t) = \left\{ g(\bar{k}(t) + \delta) - \left[\frac{\dot{L}(t)}{L(t)} + \frac{\dot{A}(t)}{A(t)} \right] (\bar{k}(t) + \delta) \right.$$
$$\left. - \dot{\bar{k}}(t) \right\} A(t) L(t). \qquad (11)$$

Now if there is a path, $\hat{k}(t)$, which commands all the parallel paths, it must make the derivative of $C(t)$ with respect to δ equal to zero for all t, assuming that $\hat{k}(t) > 0$ for all t. Taking this derivative and equating it to zero yields

$$g'(\bar{k}(t) + \delta) - \left[\frac{\dot{L}(t)}{L(t)} + \frac{\dot{A}(t)}{A(t)} \right] = 0. \qquad (12)$$

This indicates that a necessary condition for a $k(t)$ path to command all others absolutely parallel to it is that it continuously equate the marginal product of capital to the rate of growth of augmented labor. This is also a sufficient condition since *(12)* describes a unique path and the second-order condition that *(12)* describe a maximum is satisfied—both by virtue of the strict concavity of $g(k)$, i.e., diminishing marginal productivity of capital. Of course, *(12)* uniquely determines $\bar{k}(t)$ and hence the particular class of parallel paths of which one member commands all others.

I call this commanding path a Quasi-Golden Rule path for reasons indicated earlier. However this particular path is, in a certain sense, a generalization of the Golden Rule path in that the standard Golden Rule·path is a special case of the Quasi-Golden Rule path—arising if the rate of growth of augmented labor is constant.[5]

The conditions for the existence of this Quasi-Golden Rule path with $\hat{k}(t) > 0$ are entirely analogous to the conditions for the

---

[5] It may be of interest to note that, on the Quasi-Golden Rule path, investment is less than competitive profits if the augmented labor growth rate is rising, greater than profits if that growth rate is falling, and equal to profits if the augmented labor growth rate is constant. This can be shown from differentiation of *(9)*.

existence of an interior Golden Rule path. For *(9)* defines a path with $\hat{k}(t) > 0$ if and only if, for all t,

$$g'(\infty) < \frac{\dot{L}(t)}{L(t)} + \frac{\dot{A}(t)}{A(t)} < g'(0). \qquad (13)$$

If the left-hand inequality is not satisfied at some t, then no finite $\hat{k}(t)$ exists. Failure of the right-hand side inequality to be satisfied means only that the maximum is a corner maximum at $\hat{k}(t) = 0$.

Existence should not be confused with feasibility: it could be that the rate of growth of augmented labor, to which the marginal product of capital must be equated, would, over some interval of time, fall so fast as to require investment in excess of output. (This feasibility problem does not arise with the standard Golden Rule because, in that model, the rate of growth of augmented labor is constant.) But even if infeasible, this Quasi-Golden Rule path can be used to prove a theorem concerning dynamical efficiency, as will be seen in the next essay.

We have considered only absolute parallelism thus far. It is natural, at this point, to consider relative parallelism in terms of the capital-augmented labor ratio. But such parallelism is equivalent to relative parallelism in terms of the capital stock. It is economical to defer study of such parallelism to the point at which we reach the most general model considered in this paper; otherwise, we would find ourselves proving the same proposition with each extension of the model.

For the same reason, I shall not consider at this stage the analysis of commanding paths in terms of other variables such as the capital-output ratio and the rate of interest. That analysis will be conducted in the context of a much more general model.

Factor Augmentation We suppose now that technical progress is factor augmenting; positive capital augmentation is allowed. The production function takes the form

$$Q = G(BK, AL), \quad B, A > 0, \qquad (14)$$

where B and A are both increasing, continuously differentiable functions of time only. It will be supposed that, for all t,

$$\frac{\dot{L}}{L} + \frac{\dot{A}}{A} - \frac{\dot{B}}{B} > 0. \qquad (15)$$

From the equation for consumption,

$$C = G(BK, AL) - \dot{K}, \quad (16)$$

we have

$$C = \left[\frac{BG(BK, AL)}{AL} - \frac{B\dot{K}}{AL} \right] \frac{AL}{B}. \quad (17)$$

Under constant returns to scale, output per augmented labor can be expressed as a function of k, now defined as the ratio of augmented capital to augmented labor:

$$\frac{G(BK, AL)}{AL} = G\left(\frac{BK}{AL}, 1 \right) = G(k, 1) \equiv g(k), k \equiv \frac{BK}{AL}. \quad (18)$$

In these terms, the marginal product of capital is

$$\frac{\partial G(BK, AL)}{\partial K} = \frac{\partial}{\partial K} \left[AL\, G\left(\frac{BK}{AL}, 1 \right) \right]$$
$$= BG_1 \left(\frac{BK}{AL}, 1 \right) = Bg'(k). \quad (19)$$

Diminishing marginal productivity implies $g''(k) < 0$.

By differentiation of k with respect to time we have

$$\dot{k} = \frac{B\dot{K}}{AL} - \left(\frac{\dot{L}}{L} + \frac{\dot{A}}{A} - \frac{\dot{B}}{B} \right) k. \quad (20)$$

From *(17)*, *(18)*, and *(20)* we then obtain

$$C = \left[Bg(k) - \left(\frac{\dot{L}}{L} + \frac{\dot{A}}{A} - \frac{\dot{B}}{B} \right) k - \dot{k} \right] \frac{AL}{B}. \quad (21)$$

Using this equation, it can be shown, in precisely the same manner as the analogous proposition was demonstrated in the previous section, that a necessary and sufficient condition that a $k(t)$ path command all other paths absolutely parallel to it in terms of the augmented-capital–augmented-labor ratio is that, on this path, the marginal product of capital equal the rate of growth of the labor force plus the proportionate rate of "net" labor augmentation. That is, the commanding path, $\hat{k}(t)$, is defined by

$$B(t)g'(\hat{k}(t)) = \frac{\dot{L}(t)}{L(t)} + \frac{\dot{A}(t)}{A(t)} - \frac{\dot{B}(t)}{B(t)}. \quad (22)$$

This path is a Quasi-Golden Rule path in the factor-augmenting case.

The analysis of existence parallels that of the previous case. An interesting wrinkle here is that if $g'(\infty) > 0$ and $B(t) \to \infty$ as $t \to \infty$, then the left-hand side of *(22)* will eventually (if not immediately) come to exceed the right-hand side for all finite k, in which case there is no path defined (for all t) by *(22)*. The inequality $g'(\infty) > 0$ occurs if the limit of the substitution elasticity as $k \to \infty$ exceeds unity.

As for feasibility, some interesting results can be obtained if we suppose that

$$\frac{\dot{L}}{L} = \gamma, \; \frac{\dot{A}}{A} = \lambda, \; \frac{\dot{B}}{B} = \mu, \; \gamma + \lambda - \mu > 0. \qquad (23)$$

Then, by differentiation of *(22)* and using *(23)*, the definition of the investment-output ratio, s, (namely $\dot{K}/Q$) and *(20)*, we obtain

$$\hat{s} = \hat{a} + \frac{\mu \hat{\sigma}}{1 - \hat{a}} \, \hat{x}, \qquad (24)$$

where $\hat{s}$ is the investment ratio, $\hat{a}$ is capital's share, $\hat{\sigma}$ is the elasticity of substitution, and $\hat{x}$ is the capital-output ratio along the Quasi-Golden Rule path.[6] We see immediately that, given *(23)*, investment exceeds profits along this path.

Now suppose that $\sigma < 1$ for all k. Since $\hat{k}(t)$ is increasing, by *(22)*, and $\sigma < 1$, $\hat{a}$ will be decreasing. Since there is positive capital augmentation and $\sigma < 1$, progress is capital saving in Harrod's sense; therefore, $\hat{x}$ will be falling along this constant interest-rate path. If σ is bounded *below* one, then $\hat{a}$ and $\hat{x}$ will approach zero as $t \to \infty$ so that $\hat{s}$ will approach zero. If σ is not so bounded but rather $\sigma \to 1$ as $k \to \infty$, then $\hat{s}$ will approach a constant between zero and one. In either case, it is feasible, either immediately or eventually, to get onto the Quasi-Golden Rule path.

The Quasi-Golden Rule path defined in *(22)* is unsatisfying on two counts. First, the right-hand side of *(22)* could be negative, in which case this Quasi-Golden Rule path will not exist (unless $g'(k)$ turned negative for large k, contrary to our postulate).

---

[6] Use is made here of the identity $\varepsilon = -(1 - a)/\sigma$, where ε is the k-elasticity of $g'(k)$, i.e., $g''(k) \, k/g'(k)$, a negative number.

Second, in some cases at least, it is an inefficient path: the interest rate is too low, as will be seen in the next essay. We need, then, to look for other generalizations or analogues of the Golden Rule path. But, as was indicated earlier, these can best be derived in more general models.

Arbitrary Technical Progress We adopt now the most general production function used in this part of the essay, that given in *(1)*:

$$Q = F(K, L; t). \qquad (1)$$

Of course, such arbitrary technical progress includes factor augmentation as a special case so that the results of this section apply to that special case as well as other cases.

Now consumption can be expressed as

$$C = \left[\frac{F(K, L; t)}{L} - \frac{\dot{K}}{L} \right] L. \qquad (25)$$

The first term in the brackets, output per unit labor, may be written as a function of the capital-labor ratio, denoted k, and time:

$$\frac{F(K, L; t)}{L} = F\left(\frac{K}{L}, 1; t \right) \equiv f(k; t), \quad k \equiv \frac{K}{L}. \qquad (26)$$

The marginal product of capital, F_K, is equal to f_k. We also have

$$\dot{k} = \frac{\dot{K}}{L} - \frac{\dot{L}}{L} k \qquad (27)$$

whence, from *(25)*, *(26)*, and *(27)*,

$$C = \left[f(k; t) - \frac{\dot{L}}{L} k - \dot{k} \right] L. \qquad (28)$$

By analysis precisely like the foregoing, it can be shown that a necessary and sufficient condition for a growth path to command all others absolutely parallel to it in terms of the capital-labor ratio is that the path, $\hat{k}(t)$, satisfy

$$f_k(\hat{k}(t); t) = \frac{\dot{L}(t)}{L(t)}. \qquad (29)$$

That is, the marginal product of capital must equal the rate of growth of the labor force.

The analysis of the existence of this new Quasi-Golden Rule path is similar to the analysis of existence in the factor augmentation case: If $f_k(k, t)$ increases without limit as $t \to \infty$ for every k, then we require $f_k(\infty, t) = 0$ for the existence of this path.

I shall say very little about feasibility. Suppose that $\dot{L}(t)/L(t) = \gamma > 0$. Differentiating *(29)* and using *(27)*, *(29)*, and the definition of s, the investment-output ratio, we have

$$\hat{s} = \hat{a} + \left(\frac{\hat{f}_{kt}}{\hat{f}_k}\right) \frac{\hat{\sigma}}{1 - \hat{a}} \, \hat{x}. \qquad (30)$$

Hence, if $f_{kt} > 0$, which is reasonable to suppose, then investment exceeds profits on this path. If, further, technical progress is capital saving for all σ, then $\hat{x}$ and $\hat{a}$ will be falling so there is, in that case, some presumption of feasibility, at least eventually.

The reader will note that this Quasi-Golden Rule path is not a true generalization of the Golden Rule path: even if progress is purely labor augmenting and augmented labor grows exponentially, this Quasi-Golden Rule path does not reduce to the Golden Rule path. The reason is that in the Golden Rule model the paths commanded by the Golden Rule path—the other golden-age paths—exhibit *relative* parallelism in terms of the capital-(un-augmented) labor ratio, not the absolute parallelism studied here. Relative parallelism will be examined in the second half of this essay.

This Quasi-Golden Rule path, like the previous one, is inefficient in at least some cases when there is positive technical progress: it is a path on which there is excessive capital deepening. Nevertheless it is a useful tool for showing certain other paths to be inefficient, as the next essay will show.

Thus far we have been examining paths which are (absolutely) parallel in terms of the ratio of capital to labor, or augmented capital to augmented labor. It is possible to characterize paths which command all others parallel to them in terms of the *output*-labor ratio or in terms of the wage rate. But these characterizations are complex and I doubt that such analysis would be useful. Further, such concepts are necessarily restricted to models with a single kind of variable primary input (labor). We turn now to a more general model in which we study parallelism in terms of the capital stock, the marginal product of capital, and the average product of capital.

GENERALIZED GOLDEN RULE PATHS

Let us now permit the existence of many variable primary resources or kinds of labor, $L_1, L_2, \ldots, L_n$, which are taken to be continuously differentiable, nondecreasing functions of time. Our aggregative production function,

$$Q = \psi(K, L_1, L_2, \ldots, L_n; t), \qquad (31)$$

is no longer posited to be linear homogeneous in the capital and labor inputs or even homogeneous of any positive degree. But we continue to suppose that the function is twice differentiable with positive marginal products and diminishing marginal productivity of capital everywhere. There is positive technical progress for all t.[7]

Since the labor inputs are exogenous, being a function only of time, we may put the production function in the form

$$Q = P(K, t). \qquad (32)$$

The above postulates imply that, for all K and t,

$$P_K > 0, \ P_{KK} < 0, \ P_t > 0. \qquad (33)$$

I turn first to relative parallelism in terms of the capital stock.[8] I owe to Christian von Weizsäcker the suggestion that relative

[7] Note that in this model with many primary inputs, there exists generally a Golden Rule path only if *(31)* is linear homogeneous in the inputs, progress is purely primary-input augmenting, and all augmented primary inputs grow exponentially at the same rate.

[8] Note that relative parallelism in terms of the capital-labor ratio or in terms of the augmented-capital–augmented-labor ratio is equivalent to relative parallelism in terms of the capital stock. For if, as an example, the proportionate rate of change of the capital-labor ratio is the same on two paths (relative parallelism in terms of the capital-labor ratio), the proportionate rate of change of the capital stock on the two paths must also be the same (relative parallelism in terms of the capital stock), since the latter rate equals the former plus the rate of change of labor and the labor growth rate is the same on the two paths.

parallelism should be considered. Indeed, he correctly indicated that any path on which the investment ratio equals the capital elasticity of output would command all paths relatively parallel to it in terms of the capital stock. That is the "sufficiency" part of the proposition demonstrated below.

The proposition is the following. A necessary and sufficient condition that a growth path command all others relatively parallel to it in terms of the capital stock is that the investment ratio equal the capital elasticity of output (capital's competitive share under constant returns to scale), or equivalently, that the rate of growth of the capital stock equal the marginal product of capital. That is,

$$\frac{\dot{\hat{K}}}{\hat{Q}} = \frac{\hat{P}_K \hat{K}}{\hat{Q}} \qquad (34)$$

or

$$\frac{\dot{\hat{K}}}{\hat{K}} = \hat{P}_K \qquad (34a)$$

characterizes the commanding path. This will now be shown.

Consider a class of logarithmically parallel paths defined by

$$K(t) = \pi \overline{K}(t), \quad \pi > 0, \quad \overline{K}(t) > 0 \text{ for all } t, \qquad (35)$$

where $\overline{K}(t)$ is an arbitrary path, feasible or infeasible, and where π is a constant parameter greater than, equal to, or less than one. Upon noting that $\dot{K}(t) = \pi\dot{\overline{K}}(t)$ we obtain the path of consumption that corresponds to any value of π:

$$C(t) = P(\pi \overline{K}(t), t) - \pi\dot{\overline{K}}(t). \qquad (36)$$

Now if there is a path, say $\hat{K}(t)$, which commands all the others in the class of parallel paths, the derivative of $C(t)$ with respect to π must be equal to zero for all t at the value of π corresponding to that path. Hence

$$\overline{K}(t)P_K(\pi \overline{K}(t), t) - \dot{\overline{K}}(t) = 0. \qquad (37)$$

By virtue of (35), which implies $\dot{K}/K = \dot{\overline{K}}/\overline{K}$, (37) can be written

$$\frac{\dot{K}(t)}{K(t)} = P_K(K(t), t). \qquad (38)$$

This indicates that equality between the rate of growth of capital and the marginal product of capital is a necessary condition for a path to command all others logarithmically parallel to it. Further, this equality is a sufficient condition that the path described by *(38)* be a commanding path since, by virtue of diminishing marginal productivity of capital ($P_{KK} < 0$), the second-order condition that the stationary value given by *(37)* is a maximum is satisfied. (It should be clear that only if $\overline{K}(t)$ is logarithmically parallel to a path described by *(38)* does the class of logarithmically parallel paths possess a commanding path.)

It will be observed that *(34)*—and its equivalent, *(34a)*—is a differential equation in $\hat{K}(t)$: it determines a unique path if and only if the initial state, $\hat{K}(0) = K_o$, is specified. Thus *(34)* defines a whole class of commanding paths, one for each initial state.

Under what conditions does there exist a path described by *(34)*? Given any positive initial capital stock, K_o, there necessarily exists a path satisfying *(34)*.

Further, these commanding paths are necessarily feasible on our assumption of everywhere diminishing marginal product of capital. For that implies that average product of capital is falling; hence marginal product is less than average product; therefore the capital elasticity of output, to which the investment-output ratio is equated on the commanding paths, is less than unity, and so investment never exceeds output on these paths. (Also, capital never becomes negative since, by virtue of a positive marginal product of capital everywhere, capital grows from its initial positive level on any commanding path.)

I shall call these commanding paths Generalized Golden Rule paths for two reasons. First, they emerge from a fairly general model in which neither pure labor augmentation nor the existence of exactly one kind of labor nor constant returns to scale is assumed. Second, if we specialize the production function *(31)* in such a way that a Golden Rule path exists, meaning the assumption of pure labor augmentation and all the rest, then the Golden Rule path is one of these Generalized Golden Rule paths. This follows immediately from the fact that the Golden Rule path is a path on which the investment-output ratio equals the capital elasticity of output or, equivalently, the rate of growth of capital equals the marginal product of capital. A further, though inessential, property of these paths is that, as already noted, they exhibit the mystical equality between investment and competitive profits (under constant returns to scale).

It will be illuminating to express in terms of marginal and of average product of capital the differential equation that characterizes these Generalized Golden Rule paths. First, I shall let r denote the marginal product of capital; it is equal to the competitive rate of interest under constant returns to scale.

$$r = P_K(K, t). \qquad (39)$$

Upon differentiating this totally with respect to time, we obtain

$$\frac{\dot{r}}{r} = \varepsilon \frac{\dot{K}}{K} + h \qquad (40)$$

where

$$\varepsilon \equiv \frac{P_{KK}K}{P_K} < 0 \text{ [by } (33)] \text{ and } h \equiv \frac{P_{Kt}}{P_K}.$$

On any Generalized Golden Rule path we have, from $(34a)$,

$$r = \frac{\dot{K}}{K}. \qquad (41)$$

From (40) and (41) we obtain the following differential equation in r that characterizes the Generalized Golden Rule paths:

$$\frac{\dot{r}}{r} = \varepsilon \left(r - \frac{h}{-\varepsilon} \right). \qquad (42)$$

Suppose that $h > 0$; a sufficient condition for this is that the various kinds of labor are all substitutes for capital and are nondecreasing over time and that technical change is not "very" capital saving in the Hicksian sense. Suppose further that $P_K(\infty, t) = 0$, which is a frequent assumption in growth theory; then ε, which can be expressed as a function of r and t, could approach zero only as r approaches zero (for every t). On these assumptions, r will "track" or "chase" the variable $(h/-\varepsilon)$ from every initial r in the sense that r will be rising if $r < (h/-\varepsilon)$ and will be falling if $r > (h/-\varepsilon)$. However, if $P_K(\infty, t) > 0$ and $(h/-\varepsilon)$ should be below the lower bound on r, then r will merely approach its lower bound. Similarly, if $h < 0$, r will approach its lower bound.

Of special interest is the case in which $h/-\varepsilon$ is a positive constant, independent of r and t. Suppose that $P_K(\infty, t) < h/-\varepsilon$. Then one r path satisfying *(42)* is the constant r path:

$$r = \frac{h}{-\varepsilon} \cdot \qquad (43)$$

Further, if the initial r fails to satisfy *(43)* then r will approach $(h/-\varepsilon)$ asymptotically.

It will now be shown that *(43)* describes the Golden Rule path if that path exists. Assume constant returns to scale, factor augmentation, and just one labor input:

$$P(K, t) = G[B(t)K(t), A(t)L(t)]. \qquad (44)$$

Then

$$P_K(K, t) = B(t)G_1[B(t)K(t), A(t)L(t)] \qquad (45)$$

and, it can be shown,

$$\frac{P_{Kt}}{P_K} = \frac{\dot{B}}{B} + \varepsilon \left(\frac{\dot{B}}{B} - \frac{\dot{A}}{A} - \frac{\dot{L}}{L} \right) \qquad (46)$$

whence

$$\frac{h}{-\varepsilon} = \frac{\dot{A}}{A} + \frac{\dot{L}}{L} + \left(\frac{1}{-\varepsilon} - 1 \right) \frac{\dot{B}}{B} \qquad (47)$$

or, using $-\varepsilon = b/\sigma$ where b is labor's share and σ is the substitution elasticity,

$$\frac{h}{-\varepsilon} = \frac{\dot{A}}{A} + \frac{\dot{L}}{L} + \left(\frac{\sigma - b}{b} \right) \frac{\dot{B}}{B} \cdot \qquad (48)$$

Now in the Golden Rule model,

$$\frac{\dot{A}}{A} + \frac{\dot{L}}{L} = \text{constant}, \quad \frac{\dot{B}}{B} = 0, \qquad (49)$$

so we see that $(h/-\varepsilon)$ is a constant, independent of r and t, in the Golden Rule model, and that $(h/-\varepsilon)$ equals the rate of growth of augmented labor in that model. Hence *(43)* is the Golden Rule path in the Golden Rule model. Of course, in the Cobb-Douglas case, existence of the Golden Rule path does not require $\dot{B}/B = 0$ but progress is necessarily purely labor augmenting (*and* purely capital augmenting) in the Cobb-Douglas case. In this case, *(48)* gives

$$\frac{h}{-\varepsilon} = \frac{\dot{L}}{L} + \frac{\dot{A}}{A} + \frac{\alpha}{1-\alpha}\frac{\dot{B}}{B} \qquad (50)$$

where $\alpha \equiv 1 - b$, the capital exponent of the Cobb-Douglas function. Manipulation of this function shows that the sum of the last two terms in *(50)* can be regarded as the "true" rate of labor augmentation.

It should not be inferred that if $(h/-\varepsilon)$ is a constant, independent of r and t, then *(43)* is the Golden Rule path. From *(47)* we see that if

$$\frac{\dot{A}}{A} + \frac{\dot{L}}{L} = \text{constant}, \frac{\dot{B}}{B} = \text{constant}, \varepsilon = \text{constant} \quad (51)$$

then $(h/-\varepsilon)$ is a constant. Yet if $\dot{B}/B \neq 0$ and the production function is not Cobb-Douglas, then no Golden Rule path exists.[9]

The differential equation, *(34)*, that describes the class of Generalized Golden Rule paths under discussion can also be expressed in terms of the capital-output ratio, x. First, write the production function *(32)* in the form

$$P(K, t) = \eta(x, t). \qquad (52)$$

This requires only that the capital elasticity of output be less than one, which follows from everywhere diminishing returns to capital. Differentiation of

$$x = \frac{K}{Q} \qquad (53)$$

yields

$$\dot{x} = s - \frac{K}{Q}\frac{\dot{Q}}{Q} \qquad (54)$$

where $s \equiv \dot{K}/Q$, the investment-output ratio. It can be shown that

$$\frac{\dot{Q}}{Q} = \frac{a}{1-a}\frac{\dot{x}}{x} + \frac{\eta_t}{\eta} \qquad (55)$$

[9] In the constant-returns to scale, two-input, factor-augmenting case, the constant -ε production function is of the form

$$Q = a_1 AL + a_2 (BK)^{1-\beta}(AL)^\beta, \quad a_1 \geq 0, a_2 > 0, 0 < \beta < 1.$$

where a denotes the capital elasticity of output. Further, according to *(34)*, on any Generalized Golden Rule path

$$s = a. \qquad (56)$$

From *(54)*, *(55)*, and *(56)* we obtain

$$\dot{x} = \frac{(1-a)\eta_t}{\eta}\left(\frac{a}{\eta_t/\eta} - x\right). \qquad (57)$$

The analysis of this differential equation characterizing the class of Generalized Golden Rule paths is somewhat similar to the previous analysis of the differential equation in r. On certain assumptions, x will "track" the quantity $(a\eta/\eta_t)$.

Any constant x path satisfying *(57)* is one on which

$$x = \frac{a}{\eta_t/\eta} \qquad (58)$$

or equivalently

$$r = \eta_t/\eta. \qquad (59)$$

The Golden Rule path is such a path. For in the Golden Rule model, η_t/η, the rate of growth of output when the capital-output ratio is constant, equals the rate of growth of augmented labor.

I have discussed thus far only paths which command all others logarithmically parallel to them. Absolute parallelism deserves brief mention. On our assumption that the marginal product of capital is everywhere positive, there exists no path which commands all paths absolutely parallel to it in terms of the capital stock. This can be seen if we let

$$K(t) = \overline{K}(t) + \delta \qquad (60)$$

define the class of absolutely parallel paths, so that consumption is given by

$$C(t) = P[\overline{K}(t) + \delta, t] - \dot{\overline{K}}(t). \qquad (61)$$

With $P_K > 0$ for all K, the greater δ the greater is the consumption path, so there exists no path, $\overline{K}(t) + \delta$, which commands all the other parallel paths.

If the marginal product of capital equals zero on some path $\widetilde{K}(t)$ and is negative for all $K(t) > \widetilde{K}(t)$, then the path $\widetilde{K}(t)$

commands all such paths that are absolutely parallel to it in terms of the capital stock.

In the earlier model having a single primary input, we measured capital intensity in terms of the capital-labor ratio or some variant of that ratio. In the present model we have thus far worked in terms of the capital stock. Two other measures of capital intensity in the present model are the marginal product of capital and the average product of capital (or its reciprocal, the capital-output ratio). For the sake of completeness, I now analyze growth paths which command in terms of these measures of capital intensity.

Consider first absolute parallelism in terms of the marginal product of capital. Again, let r denote the marginal product of capital. The class of absolutely parallel paths is defined by

$$r(t) = \bar{r}(t) + \delta. \qquad (62)$$

Hence the $K(t)$ path corresponding to any $r(t)$ path in this class of paths is determined by

$$\bar{r} + \delta = P_K(K, t). \qquad (63)$$

Differentiating totally with respect to time, we obtain

$$\dot{K} = \frac{\dot{\bar{r}}}{P_{KK}} - K \frac{P_{Kt}}{P_K} \cdot \frac{P_K}{P_{KK}K} \qquad (64)$$

or

$$\dot{K} = \frac{\dot{\bar{r}}}{P_{KK}} - \frac{Kh}{\varepsilon}. \qquad (64a)$$

Partial differentiation of *(63)* with respect to δ yields

$$\frac{\partial \dot{K}}{\partial \delta} = \frac{1}{P_{KK}} < 0. \qquad (65)$$

Upon differentiating *(64a)* partially with respect to δ we obtain

$$\frac{\partial \dot{K}}{\partial \delta} = \left\{ -\frac{P_{KKK}\dot{\bar{r}}}{(P_{KK})^2} - \frac{h}{\varepsilon} \right.$$
$$\left. - K \left[\frac{(\partial h/\partial K)\varepsilon - (\partial \varepsilon/\partial K)h}{\varepsilon^2} \right] \right\} \frac{\partial K}{\partial \delta} \qquad (66)$$

or equivalently,

$$\frac{\partial \dot{K}}{\partial \delta} = \left\{ -E(P_{KK}) \frac{1}{\varepsilon} \frac{\dot{\bar{r}}}{\bar{r} + \delta} - \frac{h}{\varepsilon} - \frac{h}{\varepsilon} [E(h) - E(\varepsilon)] \right\} \frac{\partial K}{\partial \delta} \quad (66a)$$

where $E(y)$ denotes the K-elasticity of any variable y:

$$E(y) = \frac{(\partial y/\partial K)K}{y}.$$

Using the consumption relation

$$C = P(K, t) - \dot{K} \quad (67)$$

we have

$$\frac{\partial C}{\partial \delta} = \frac{\partial P}{\partial K} \frac{\partial K}{\partial \delta} - \frac{\partial \dot{K}}{\partial \delta}. \quad (68)$$

Now if there exists a path $\bar{r}(t) + \delta$ which commands all the other parallel paths, that path must make $\partial C/\partial \delta = 0$, assuming that an interior maximum occurs. Substituting *(63)* for $\partial P/\partial K$ and *(66a)* for $\partial \dot{K}/\partial \delta$ we obtain

$$\frac{\partial C}{\partial \delta} = \left\{ (\bar{r} + \delta) + \frac{h}{\varepsilon} + \frac{h}{\varepsilon} [E(h) - E(\varepsilon)] \right.$$
$$\left. + E(P_{KK}) \frac{1}{\varepsilon} \frac{\dot{\bar{r}}}{\bar{r} + \delta} \right\} \frac{\partial K}{\partial \delta}. \quad (69)$$

Setting this derivative equal to zero, noting that $\partial K/\partial \delta < 0$ for all K and t, and writing $\hat{r}(t)$ for $\bar{r}(t) + \delta$, the commanding path, yields

$$\frac{\dot{\hat{r}}}{\hat{r}} = \frac{\varepsilon}{-E(P_{KK})} \left\{ \hat{r} - \frac{h}{-\varepsilon} - \frac{h}{-\varepsilon} [E(h) - E(\varepsilon)] \right\}. \quad (70)$$

Any path which commands all others absolutely parallel to it in terms of the marginal product of capital must satisfy *(70)*. Hence *(70)* is a necessary condition of command in this respect. However *(70)* is a sufficient condition only if the second-order condition is satisfied; even then there may be local maxima so that not every path satisfying *(70)* commands *all* other parallel paths. In fact, the second-order condition, $\partial^2 C/\partial \delta^2 < 0$ is not necessarily satisfied; the algebraic sign of this derivative depends upon the signs of such quantities as $E(h)$ and $\partial E(h)/\partial \delta$ which can be of either sign.

Of course, the Golden Rule path (if the model is such as to permit its existence) satisfies *(70)*. In the Golden Rule model, as was shown earlier, $(h/-\varepsilon)$ is the rate of growth of augmented labor; it is a constant, independent of K and t. Hence, in that model, $E(h) - E(\varepsilon) = 0$, so that the Golden Rule path $r = (h/-\varepsilon) = $ constant satisfies *(70)*.

Consider now relative parallelism in terms of the marginal product of capital. The class of logarithmically parallel paths is defined by

$$r(t) = \pi \bar{r}(t), \quad \bar{r}(t) > 0 \text{ for all } t, \qquad (71)$$

so that

$$\pi \bar{r}(t) = P_K(K, t) \qquad (72)$$

determines the $K(t)$ path associated with any of these parallel paths.

Then, by differentiation of *(72)*

$$\dot{K} = \frac{\pi \dot{\bar{r}}}{P_{KK}} - \frac{Kh}{\varepsilon} \qquad (73)$$

and

$$\frac{\partial K}{\partial \pi} = \frac{\bar{r}}{P_{KK}} < 0. \qquad (74)$$

From *(73)*

$$\frac{\partial \dot{K}}{\partial \pi} = \frac{\dot{\bar{r}}}{P_{KK}} \cdot \frac{\partial \pi}{\partial K} \cdot \frac{\partial K}{\partial \pi} + \left\{ -\frac{P_{KKK} \pi \dot{\bar{r}}}{(P_{KK})^2} \right.$$

$$\left. -\frac{h}{\varepsilon} - \frac{h}{\varepsilon} [E(h) - E(\varepsilon)] \right\} \frac{\partial K}{\partial \pi} \qquad (75)$$

$$= \left\{ \frac{\dot{\bar{r}}}{\bar{r}} \left[1 - \frac{E(P_{KK})}{\varepsilon} \right] - \frac{h}{\varepsilon} - \frac{h}{\varepsilon} [E(h) - E(\varepsilon)] \right\} \frac{\partial K}{\partial \pi}.$$

From the consumption relation we then obtain

$$\frac{\partial C}{\partial \pi} = \left\{ \pi \bar{r} + \frac{h}{\varepsilon} + \frac{h}{\varepsilon} [E(h) - E(\varepsilon)] \right.$$

$$\left. + \left[\frac{E(P_{KK})}{\varepsilon} - 1 \right] \frac{\dot{\bar{r}}}{\bar{r}} \right\} \frac{\partial K}{\partial \pi}. \qquad (76)$$

Equating this derivative to zero and writing $\hat{r}(t)$ for $\pi\bar{r}(t)$, the commanding path, we have

$$\frac{\dot{\hat{r}}}{\hat{r}} = \frac{\varepsilon}{\varepsilon - E(P_{KK})} \left\{ \hat{r} - \frac{h}{-\varepsilon} - \frac{h}{-\varepsilon} [E(h) - E(\varepsilon)] \right\}. \quad (77)$$

This is only a necessary condition. Once again, the second-order conditions for a maximum may not be satisfied.

Let us turn finally to parallelism in terms of the capital-output ratio. From the relations

$$Q = \eta(x, t) \quad (78)$$

and

$$K = xQ \quad (79)$$

we obtain

$$\dot{K} = \frac{Q}{b} \dot{x} + HK \quad (80)$$

where

$$H \equiv \frac{\eta_t(x, t)}{\eta(x, t)}, \ b \equiv 1 - a.$$

H is the rate of growth of output when the capital-output ratio is constant.

Now consider the class of absolutely parallel paths

$$x(t) = \bar{x}(t) + \delta. \quad (81)$$

Regarding b and H as functions of K and t, we obtain from *(80)*

$$\frac{\partial \dot{K}}{\partial \delta} = \left[\frac{1}{b} \left(\frac{P_K K}{P} - \frac{b_K K}{b} \right) \frac{\dot{\bar{x}}}{\bar{x} + \delta} + H \left(1 + \frac{H_K K}{H} \right) \right] \frac{\partial K}{\partial \delta} \quad (82)$$

$$= \left[\frac{1}{b} (a - E(b)) \frac{\dot{\bar{x}}}{\bar{x} + \delta} + H(1 + E(H)) \right] \frac{\partial K}{\partial \delta}$$

where $\partial K/\partial \delta = Q/b > 0$. Hence, using the consumption relation, we have

$$\frac{\partial C}{\partial \delta} = \left\{ P_K - \left[H(1 + E(H)) + \frac{1}{b} (a - E(b)) \right] \right\} \frac{\partial K}{\partial \delta}. \quad (83)$$

Equating this derivative to zero and letting $\hat{x}(t)$ denote $\bar{x}(t) + \delta$, we have

$$\frac{\dot{\hat{x}}}{\hat{x}} = \frac{b}{a - E(b)} \{ P_K - H[1 + E(H)] \}. \quad (84)$$

This is a necessary condition that the path $\hat{x}(t)$ be commanding. It is not a sufficient condition on our previous assumptions; the second-order conditions for a maximum need not be satisfied. Note that *(84)* is somewhat symmetrical to *(70)*.

The Golden Rule path satisfies *(84)*. In the Golden Rule model, H measures the growth rate of augmented labor and $E(H) = 0$. On the Golden Rule path, $P_K = H$ and $\dot{x} = 0$.

Analysis of relative parallelism in terms of the capital-output ratio will yield an equation somewhat like *(84)*. Again, the second-order conditions are not necessarily satisfied on present assumptions.

We have, in the second part of this essay, considered a number of paths which, on certain assumptions, can be regarded as generalizations of the Golden Rule path. In each case, the Golden Rule path is a special case of the Generalized Golden Rule path. The commanding paths in terms of the marginal and average product of capital cannot be characterized simply; in addition, the second-order conditions are cumbersome and difficult to interpret. It will not be surprising, therefore, that the first of the Generalized Golden Rule paths—that on which the investment ratio equals the capital elasticity of output—is the most useful. It is time—high time, the reader will no doubt think—that we examine the uses to which the Golden Rule path and its generalizations can be put.

An Essay on
Dynamical Efficiency

When the several discoverers of the Golden Rule published their results, question naturally arose as to the normative significance of the theorem. I called the saving rule which prevails on the consumption-maximizing golden-age path the Golden Rule of Accumulation because, on that path, each "generation" saves (on behalf of future generations as it were) that fraction of income which it would have past generations save for it, subject to the constraint that all generations past and present are to save the same fraction of income. But while such a line of thought may sometime offer a clue to an ethically satisfying rule of saving, no proof—indeed, no criterion—of "optimality" of the Golden Rule path or of asymptotic approach to it from historically given initial conditions was given in my paper and the others, nor was any suggestion of optimality seriously intended. One can imagine optimality criteria such that society will not aim to achieve golden-age growth asymptotically. And even if, upon application of the Ramsey social utility criterion, some golden-age path should be utility maximizing (for some initial conditions), the rate of time preference may make that path different from the Golden Rule path.[1] It was evidently reflections such as these that led Ivor Pearce and Paul Samuelson to doubt that the Golden Rule notion has any important normative significance.[2]

[1] An application of the Golden Rule notion to the solution of the "Ramsey problem" in a growing economy and a discussion of the relation between the Golden Rule path and the "optimal" growth path is contained in the next essay.

[2] I. F. Pearce, "The End of the Golden Age in Solovia," *American Economic Review*, Vol. 52 (December 1962), pp. 1088–1097; P. A. Samuelson, "Comment," *Review of Economic Studies*, Volume 29 (June 1962), pp. 251–254.

This essay shows, however, that whether or not it is "optimal" on some criterion, the Golden Rule path does have the following important normative property: any growth path on which, at some point in time and forever after, the capital-output ratio (or capital-augmented labor ratio) always exceeds its Golden Rule level by at least some constant amount—equivalently, any path which eventually keeps the social rate of return to investment (or competitive rate of interest) permanently below its Golden Rule value by at least some finite amount—is *dynamically inefficient* in the sense that there will exist another path which, starting from the same initial capital stock, "dominates" the former path—i.e., yields more consumption at least some of the time and never less consumption. The significance of the theorem is this: no path which is dynamically inefficient can be optimal; hence no path which transgresses the Golden Rule path in the manner described can be optimal.[3] (The reader is warned that it is only paths which so transgress the Golden Rule path for *infinitely long time* that can be shown to be dynamically inefficient.)

Since the conditions for the existence of the Golden Rule path are stringent, this theorem is only of theoretical interest. But analogous theorems are proved for models in which no golden-age paths, and hence no Golden Rule path, need exist. (In particular, application is made of a Generalized Golden Rule path in the second part of this essay.) Thus it is shown that the possibility of excessive capital deepening despite *a continuously positive rate of interest* is quite general in economies that are forever growing.

APPLICATION OF THE GOLDEN RULE AND QUASI-GOLDEN RULE PATHS

From the Golden Rule model one can show immediately that some golden-age paths are dynamically inefficient. Consider any golden-age path on which the capital-output ratio (or capital-augmented labor ratio) forever exceeds its Golden Rule value. This path will be dominated, for example, by a policy of immediately gobbling up the "excess" capital and forever after main-

---

[3] This statement requires some qualification if there is uncertainty, as a later footnote indicates.

taining the capital-output ratio at its Golden Rule value, i.e., following the Golden Rule path. For such a policy will clearly give a consumption "bonus" initially (as the excess capital is consumed) and thereafter uniformly higher consumption since the Golden Rule path is the consumption-maximizing golden-age path.

In the author's reply to Pearce an obvious generalization of this result to *non*-golden age paths was conjectured: "Any policy which causes the capital-output ratio [equivalently, the capital-augmented labor ratio, since the one ratio is a monotonically increasing function of the other] permanently to exceed—always by some minimum finite amount—its Golden Rule level is inefficient and hence cannot be optimal."[4] A proof of this conjecture was later communicated to the author by Tjalling Koopmans. In this part of the paper we present what is essentially Koopmans's proof and then employ the technique to prove analogous theorems for the case of general factor-augmenting technical progress and for the case of arbitrary technical progress. The analysis is confined to the neoclassical production function, although the theorems proved carry over to the fixed-proportions (Harrod-Domar) production function.

Pure Labor Augmentation at a Constant Rate Our neoclassical production function is of the form

$$Q(t) = F[K(t), e^{\lambda t}L(t)], \quad \lambda > 0 \qquad (1)$$

with constant returns to scale, twice differentiability, and everywhere positive and diminishing marginal productivities, where Q is output, K is capital, L is labor, and t is time. Hence we may write

$$\frac{Q(t)}{e^{\lambda t}L(t)} = f(k(t)), \; f'(k) > 0, \; f''(k) < 0, \qquad (2)$$

where

$$k(t) = \frac{K(t)}{e^{\lambda t}L(t)}$$

and

$$f(k(t)) = F[k(t), 1].$$

[4] E. S. Phelps, "The End of the Golden Age in Solovia: Comment," *American Economic Review*, Vol. 52 (December 1962), pp. 1097–1099.

The derivative $f'(k)$ is the marginal product of capital. The variable k is the capital-augmented labor ratio.

The labor force increases exponentially at rate γ:

$$L(t) = L_o e^{\gamma t} \quad \gamma > 0. \qquad (3)$$

(It is really essential only that augmented labor grow exponentially.)

Neglecting depreciation (or interpreting F as a net product function) we have for consumption, C, the following relation:

$$C(t) = F[K(t), e^{(\gamma+\lambda)t}L_o] - \dot{K}(t) \qquad (4)$$

where $\dot{K}(t)$ denotes the absolute time rate of increase of capital and is hence the rate of investment. Upon dividing *(4)* by $L_o e^{(\gamma+\lambda)t}$ and using *(2)* we have

$$\frac{C(t)}{L_o e^{(\gamma+\lambda)t}} = f(k(t)) - \frac{\dot{K}(t)}{L_o e^{(\gamma+\lambda)t}}. \qquad (5)$$

Differentiating $k(t)$ with respect to time yields

$$\dot{k}(t) = \frac{\dot{K}}{L_o e^{(\gamma+\lambda)t}} - (\gamma + \lambda) \frac{K(t)}{L_o e^{(\gamma+\lambda)t}}. \qquad (6)$$

Equations *(5)* and *(6)* then yield the desired relation between consumption, the capital-augmented labor ratio, and its rate of change:

$$C(t) = [f(k(t)) - (\gamma + \lambda)k(t) - \dot{k}(t)]L_o e^{(\gamma+\lambda)t}. \qquad (7)$$

Assume now that there exists a Golden Rule path, hence a Golden Rule value of k, say $\hat{k}$. For simplicity only, we assume that the Golden Rule maximum is an interior one. Hence, as was shown in the first essay and as can be seen by equating the derivative (for fixed k) of $C(t)$ in *(7)* equal to zero, $\hat{k}$ is determined by the equation

$$f'(\hat{k}) = \gamma + \lambda. \qquad (8)$$

As a consequence of *(2)*, the expression $f(k) - (\gamma + \lambda)k$ appearing in *(7)* is monotonically increasing in k up to $k = \hat{k}$ and monotonically decreasing in k for all $k > \hat{k}$.

Consider now any growth path which "violates" the Golden Rule in the following way: at some point in time (perhaps initially) and forever thereafter, it keeps the capital-augmented labor ratio in excess of its Golden Rule value $\hat{k}$ by at least some positive, constant amount, say ϵ. That is, consider any path $k(t)$ such that, for all $t \geq t_0 \geq 0$,

$$k(t) \geq \hat{k} + \epsilon, \quad \epsilon > 0 \text{ and independent of } t. \tag{9}$$

Then the following theorem can be proved:

> *Any path satisfying (9) is "dynamically inefficient" for there always exists another path which, starting from the same initial capital stock, provides more consumption at least some of the time and never less consumption.*

Proof: Define a "comparison" path, $k^*(t)$, such that

$$k^*(t) = \begin{cases} k(t), & 0 \leq t < t_0; \\ k(t) - \epsilon, & t \geq t_0. \end{cases} \tag{10}$$

In the first interval, $0 \leq t < t_0$, the two paths are identical so that $C^*(t) = C(t)$ in this interval (which will not exist if $t_0 = 0$). At $t = t_0$, the comparison or starred path gives a discontinuous consumption bonus, for an amount of capital per augmented labor equal to ϵ is instantly consumed so as to make $k^*(t) = k(t) - \epsilon$ at $t = t_0$. In the remaining interval, $t > t_0$, the difference between the consumption rate offered by the starred path and the path specified in *(9)* is implied by *(7)* to be

$$C^*(t) - C(t) = \{[f(k^*(t)) - (\gamma + \lambda)k^*(t) - \dot{k}^*(t)] \\ - [f(k(t)) - (\gamma + \lambda)k(t) - \dot{k}(t)]\}L_o e^{(\gamma+\lambda)t}. \tag{11}$$

But observe that, for all $t > t_0$, $\dot{k}^*(t) = \dot{k}(t)$ since the two paths differ after t_0 by only a constant, ϵ. Hence *(10)* and *(11)* imply

$$C^*(t) - C(t) = \{[f(k^*(t)) - (\gamma + \lambda)k^*(t)] \\ - [f(k(t)) - (\gamma + \lambda)k(t)]\}L_o e^{(\gamma+\lambda)t}. \tag{12}$$

The right-hand side of *(12)* is strictly positive for all $t > t_0$ since $k^*(t) \geq \hat{k}$, $k(t) > k^*(t)$, and $f(k) - (\gamma + \lambda)k$ is strictly decreasing in k for $k > \hat{k}$. Hence, in the interval $t > t_0$, the starred path gives more consumption at every point in time. Therefore, the starred path dominates the other path for it is never worse and is better for all $t \geq t_0$. Q.E.D.

To elaborate a little on the last step of the proof, note that $k^*(t) \geq \hat{k}$ because $k^*(t)$ is only ϵ smaller than $k(t)$ and the latter is at least ϵ larger than $\hat{k}$ for all t. Figure 3 illustrates why

FIGURE 3

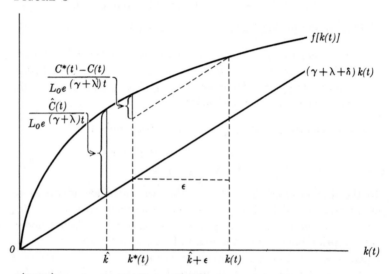

$f(k^*(t)) - (\gamma + \lambda)k^*(t) > f(k(t)) - (\gamma + \lambda)k(t)$ for any $t > t_0$.

The theorem can be expressed in another way. Since the social net rate of return to investment (and the competitive rate of interest), $f'(k(t))$, is a monotonically decreasing function of $k(t)$ and independent of time, an equivalent proposition is that any growth path which keeps the rate of return to investment forever and finitely below its Golden Rule value (the golden-age growth rate) is dynamically inefficient. Or the proposition can be expressed in terms of the capital-output ratio, as I first conjectured it.

Another remark is that the neoclassical assumptions $f'(k) > 0$ and $f''(k) < 0$ for all k are far stronger than necessary for the theorem. If $f''(k) = 0$ for all $k > \hat{k}$, for example (where $\hat{k}$ is now defined as the smallest k for which $f'(k) = (\gamma + \lambda + \delta)$), then, while the two paths will yield the same consumption path after t_0, the starred path still offers the consumption bonus at t_0, and hence dominates the other path. Secondly, the theorem is trivial in the Harrod-Domar case, where $f'(k) = 0$ for $k > \hat{k}$, for it simply means that any path which keeps capital permanently in surplus is inefficient, and this hardly needs proving.

We have been discussing here a *sufficient* condition for dynamical inefficiency in the Golden Rule model. We have not completely characterized the class of dynamically inefficient growth paths in this model. In particular, *(9)* is not a necessary condition for inefficiency. For example, as David Cass and Menahem Yaari[5] have pointed out, any path which starts with a capital stock above the Golden Rule level at $t = 0$ and causes consumption per augmented labor to equal the Golden Rule consumption level for all $t \geq 0$ is also inefficient even though such a path causes $k(t) \to \hat{k}$ as $t \to \infty$; for this consumption policy passes up the opportunity for a consumption bonus at $t = 0$.[6]

General Factor Augmentation   Let us continue to suppose that technical progress is factor augmenting. But we drop the assumption that the rate of labor augmentation is necessarily constant over time. In addition we allow progress to be partially or even wholly capital augmenting. Finally, we permit the rate of growth of the labor force to be variable over time. As a consequence of these generalizations, no Golden Rule path exists (except in the special case that the present model is identical to the previous model).

Our neoclassical production function is now

$$Q(t) = F[B(t)K(t), A(t)L(t)] \qquad (13)$$

where $A(t)$, $B(t)$, and $L(t)$ are continuously differentiable functions of time. Then output per augmented labor is given by

$$\frac{Q(t)}{A(t)L(t)} = f(k(t)), \; f'(k) > 0, \; f''(k) < 0 \qquad (14)$$

[5] D. Cass and M. E. Yaari, "Individual Saving, Aggregate Capital Formation and Economic Growth," Cowles Foundation Discussion, Paper No. 198 (December 1965).

[6] It is true however that $k(t) > \hat{k}$ for all t is not a sufficient condition for a path $k(t)$ to be dominated by the kind of comparison path used in the preceding analysis. For a discussion of this matter see Footnote 11 in E. S. Phelps, "Second Essay on the Golden Rule of Accumulation," *American Economic Review*, Vol. 55 (September 1965), pp. 793–814.

where

$$k(t) = \frac{B(t)K(t)}{A(t)L(t)}$$

and $f(k(t)) = F[k(t), 1]$. The quantity $B(t)f'(k(t))$ is the marginal product of capital.

From the consumption relation

$$C(t) + \dot{K}(t) = A(t)L(t)f(k(t)) \qquad (15)$$

and

$$\dot{k}(t) = \frac{B(t)\dot{K}(t)}{A(t)L(t)} - \left[\frac{\dot{L}(t)}{L(t)} + \frac{\dot{A}(t)}{A(t)} - \frac{\dot{B}(t)}{B(t)}\right]k(t), \qquad (16)$$

we obtain the following expression for consumption in terms of $k(t)$:

$$C(t) = \left\{B(t)f(k(t)) - \left[\frac{\dot{L}(t)}{L(t)} + \frac{\dot{A}(t)}{A(t)} - \frac{\dot{B}(t)}{B(t)}\right]k(t) - \dot{k}(t)\right\}$$
$$\times \frac{A(t)L(t)}{B(t)}. \qquad (17)$$

As discussed in the previous essay, there may exist in this general factor-augmentation case a Quasi-Golden Rule path, say $\hat{k}(t)$, which "commands" all other paths which are absolutely parallel to it in terms of the augmented-capital–augmented-labor ratio, k. If this maximum is an interior one, this Quasi-Golden Rule path is defined by

$$B(t)f'(\hat{k}(t)) = \frac{\dot{L}(t)}{L(t)} + \frac{\dot{A}(t)}{A(t)} - \frac{\dot{B}(t)}{B(t)}. \qquad (18)$$

We assume now that the path defined in *(18)* exists.

It can now be shown, in precisely the same manner as the previous theorem was shown, that this Quasi-Golden Rule path has the following property: any path which, at some point in time and forever after, keeps the ratio of augmented capital to augmented labor in excess of $\hat{k}(t)$ by at least some positive, constant amount ϵ is dynamically inefficient. That is, any path is inefficient which causes $k(t)$ to satisfy, for all $t \geq t_0 \geq 0$,

$$k(t) \geq \hat{k}(t) + \epsilon, \quad \epsilon > 0 \text{ and constant.} \qquad (19)$$

The proof shows that the following comparison path dominates any such path:

$$k^*(t) = \begin{cases} k(t), & 0 \le t < t_0; \\ k(t) - \epsilon, & \ge t_0. \end{cases} \qquad (20)$$

Comparing the associated consumption paths, we observe that they yield identical consumption until t_0. At this point the starred path yields a consumption bonus, unlike the other path in *(19)*. Subsequently, $\dot{k}^*(t) = \dot{k}(t)$ since, for $t > t_0$, $k^*(t)$ and $k(t)$ differ by a constant. It then follows, upon expressing $C^*(t) - C(t)$ in terms of $k^*(t)$ and $k(t)$ from *(17)*, that $C^*(t) - C(t) > 0$ for all $t > t_0$ as in the previous theorem.

It was mentioned that the theorem on page 59 could be reformulated in terms of paths that keep the rate of return to investment or competitive interest rate finitely below its Golden Rule value. In the present model, it is not possible with full generality to say that all paths are inefficient which keep the rate of return finitely below the Quasi-Golden Rule rate of return, $B(t)f'\big(\hat{k}(t)\big)$, as given in *(18)*.[7]

Arbitrary Technical Progress Of course, this case includes factor augmentation as a special case. But the Quasi-Golden Rule applied here in the identification of dynamically inefficient paths is different from the previous Quasi-Golden Rule path, which exists only if technical progress is factor augmenting. (The difference is due to the difference in "parallelism" used to derive the paths.)

---

[7] If there is capital augmenting progress and $B(t) \to \infty$ as $t \to \infty$, then the theorem of this section does not imply that all paths which keep the interest rate finitely below the Quasi-Golden Rule value are dynamically inefficient. To see this, consider a path such that $r(t) \le \hat{r}(t) - \eta$, $\eta > 0$, where $r(t) = B(t)f'(k(t))$ and $\hat{r}(t) = B(t)f'(\hat{k}(t)) = (\dot{L}(t)/L(t) + \dot{A}(t)/A(t)) - (\dot{B}(t)/B(t))$. Then $f'(\hat{k}(t)) - f'(k(t)) \ge \eta/B(t)$. If $B(t) \to \infty$ as $t \to \infty$ then, while $k(t) > \hat{k}(t)$ for all t, $k(t) - \hat{k}(t) \to 0$ as $t \to \infty$ is possible. Hence "$k(t) \ge \hat{k}(t) + \epsilon$, $\epsilon > 0$" is not necessarily true of such a path, so the inefficiency of all such low-interest-rate paths is not implied.

However it can be shown, at least on certain simplifying assumptions, that finite interest rate differences do imply finite $k(t)$ differences in the limit if $k(t)$ is bounded above zero on the interest-rate paths.

We write the neoclassical production function in the form

$$Q(t) = F[K(t), L(t); t] \qquad (21)$$

or, by constant returns to scale,

$$\frac{Q(t)}{L(t)} = f(k(t); t), \; f_k(k; t) > 0, \; f_{kk}(k; t) < 0 \qquad (22)$$

where

$$k(t) = \frac{K(t)}{L(t)}$$

and

$$f(k(t); t) = F[k(t), 1; t].$$

From the consumption relation

$$C(t) + \dot{K}(t) = L(t)f(k(t); t) \qquad (23)$$

and

$$\dot{k}(t) = \frac{\dot{K}(t)}{L(t)} - \frac{\dot{L}(t)}{L(t)} k(t) \qquad (24)$$

we obtain

$$C(t) = [f(k(t); t) - \frac{\dot{L}(t)}{L(t)} k(t) - \dot{k}(t)]L(t). \qquad (25)$$

As indicated in the previous essay, there may exist a Quasi-Golden Rule path which, if there is an interior maximum, is defined by

$$f_k(\hat{k}(t); t) = \frac{\dot{L}(t)}{L(t)}. \qquad (26)$$

This path "commands" all others absolutely parallel to it in terms of the capital-labor ratio, k.

It can be shown, by the same methods we have been using, that any path which, at some $t_0 \geq 0$ and forever after, causes $k(t)$ to satisfy

$$k(t) \geq \hat{k}(t) + \epsilon, \quad \epsilon > 0 \text{ and constant}, \qquad (27)$$

is dominated by the comparison path,

$$k^*(t) = \begin{cases} k(t), & 0 \leq t < t_0 \\ k(t) - \epsilon, & t \geq t_0, \end{cases} \qquad (28)$$

so that such a path is dynamically inefficient.[8]

Suppose that technical progress is factor augmenting so that while *(21)* remains valid, it is possible to write $F(K, L; t)$ in the form $G(BK, AL)$ as in *(13)*. Then if the paths defined by *(18)* and *(26)* exist, we have two Quasi-Golden Rule paths. Is it the case that one of these is efficient and the other inefficient? If the interest-rate path on one of these Quasi-Golden Rule paths were uniformly below the other (eventually) then there would be some presumption that the "low-interest" path was inefficient; but the preceding two footnotes warn against any simple translation of our theorems into statements about interest rates. I believe there is a wide class of cases in which both Quasi-Golden Rule paths are dynamically inefficient. For suppose that $\dot{L}(t) = 0$ and that $\dot{A}(t)/A(t) \leq \dot{B}(t)/B(t)$. Then interest rates are nonpositive on both paths. Yet, if there is positive technical progress (in the sense $F_t > 0$) and technical progress is not "very capital saving" (in the sense $F_{Kt} < 0$), then there is some presumption that a zero interest-rate path is dynamically inefficient. (In any case, a path with a *negative* competitive interest rate, even over some finite interval of time, is inefficient, for a negative social rate of return implies the possibility of more consumption today and tomorrow, consumption in all other periods held constant.) The second part of this essay, which applies a Generalized Golden Rule path to the analysis of dynamical inefficiency, lends some support to this presumption.

APPLICATION OF A GENERALIZED GOLDEN RULE PATH

We now allow the existence of many primary inputs and even the possibility of nonconstant returns to scale. Our production function is of the form

$$Q(t) = P[K(t), t], \quad P_K(K, t) > 0, \quad P_{KK}(K, t) < 0, \\ P_t(K, t) > 0. \qquad (29)$$

---

[8] Is any path which keeps the competitive interest rate finitely below $\dot{L}(t)/L(t)$ necessarily inefficient? In this case as in the factor-augmenting case, finite interest-rate differences need not imply finite $k(t)$ differences in the limit as $t \to \infty$. For example, the marginal productivity schedule $f_k(k; t)$ plotted against k may approach a stationary vertical line.

Consider now a path which satisfies, for all $t \geq t_0 \geq 0$,

$$K(t) \geq (1 + \epsilon)\hat{K}(t), \quad \epsilon > 0 \text{ and constant,} \qquad (30)$$

where $\hat{K}(t)$ is any path satisfying

$$\frac{\dot{\hat{K}}(t)}{\hat{K}(t)} = P_K[\hat{K}(t), t], \quad t \geq 0. \qquad (31)$$

Equation *(31)* characterizes the family of Generalized Golden Rule paths of a type discussed in the preceding essay. Every path satisfying *(31)*—there is one such path for every initial $K(0)$—has the Golden Rule-like property that it commands all paths logarithmically parallel to it in terms of the capital stock.

It should be noted that any path which satisfies *(30)* "violates" the specified Generalized Golden Rule path in the same way as any path satisfying *(9)* in the first section of this essay "violates" the Golden Rule path; for any path which satisfies *(9)* makes the ratio of $K(t)$ to the Golden Rule capital stock, $L_o e^{(\gamma+\lambda)t}\hat{k}$, at least as great as one plus some positive constant.

Since any path satisfying *(9)* has been shown to be inefficient, it is natural to conjecture that any path satisfying *(30)* is likewise dynamically inefficient. The trick, of course, is to find the proper comparison path, which proved somewhat elusive for the present author. Fortunately, David Cass has produced the following proof of this conjecture.

Define the following comparison path, $K^*(t)$, in terms of given $K(t)$ and $\hat{K}(t)$:

$$K^*(t) = \begin{cases} K(t), & 0 \leq t < t_0; \\ K(t) - \epsilon\hat{K}(t), & t \geq t_0. \end{cases} \qquad (32)$$

This comparison path gives the same consumption stream until t_0 at which time it gives a consumption bonus equal to ϵ. Thereafter, for all $t \geq t_0$, we have the difference

$$
\begin{aligned}
C^*(t) - C(t) &= \{P[K^*(t), t] - \dot{K}^*(t)\} - \{P[K(t), t] - \dot{K}(t)\} \\
&= P[K(t) - \epsilon\hat{K}(t), t] - P[K(t), t] + \epsilon\dot{\hat{K}}(t) \\
&> -P_K[K(t) - \epsilon\hat{K}(t), t]\epsilon\hat{K}(t) \qquad (33) \\
&\quad + P_K[\hat{K}(t), t]\epsilon\hat{K}(t) \\
&\geq 0.
\end{aligned}
$$

The first (strict) inequality follows, first, from the fact that $P_K[\hat{K}(t), t]\epsilon\hat{K}(t) = \epsilon\dot{\hat{K}}(t)$, by virtue of *(31)*, and, second, from the strict concavity assumption in *(29)*, $P_{KK} < 0$, which implies that $P[K(t), t] - P[K(t) - \epsilon\hat{K}(t), t] < P_K[K(t) - \epsilon\hat{K}(t), t]$. The second inequality follows from *(29)* and *(30)* which state concavity of P in K and $K(t) - \epsilon\hat{K}(t) \geq \hat{K}(t)$.

Under certain assumptions on the rate and factor-saving character of technical progress (like $P_{Kt} > 0$), the zero interest-rate path and many positive interest-rate paths will cause $K(t)$ to satisfy *(30)* and hence, by implication of the preceding theorem, be dynamically inefficient. Once again, then, we see the possibility of dynamical inefficiency despite a continuously positive rate of return to investment.

As in the first part of this essay, a complete characterization of the class of dynamically inefficient (and hence efficient) paths has not been accomplished. It seems likely that *(30)* is not a necessary condition for inefficiency in the present model. For example, paths which cycle endlessly around some Generalized Golden Rule path may also be inefficient if they cause $K(t)$ to "average" above $\hat{K}(t)$ in some sense. But probably the set of necessary and sufficient conditions for dynamical efficiency will involve the concept of the Generalized Golden Rule.

CONCLUDING REMARKS

It has been shown here that any growth path which permanently deepens capital in excess of the Golden Rule path by at least some nonvanishing amount is dynamically inefficient—it is dominated with respect to consumption by another path. If labor augmentation or labor-force growth is nonexponential or if technical progress cannot be described as purely labor augmenting, then, while no Golden Rule path will exist, there may still exist Quasi-Golden Rule paths having the same property, namely, that any permanent capital deepening in excess of such a path is dynamically inefficient. Finally, whether or not a Quasi-Golden Rule path exists, there will exist Generalized Golden Rule paths having the same normative property. Hence, the usual conditions for statical efficiency together with a continuously nonnegative rate of return to investment are not sufficient for dynamical efficiency.

Concerning the significance of these findings, I believe that it is of considerable theoretical interest to understand better the nature of excessive capital deepening. The practical importance of these findings is arguable. Beware of the weakness of what has been proved here. On the growth paths shown here to be dynamically inefficient, the capital stock is excessive *forever*. Whatever a nation does over a finite time, provided it keeps the rate of return to investment nonnegative, cannot be shown to be dynamically inefficient in the sense of this essay; for what the nation does subsequently may save the entire growth path from being dominated.[9]   At best, the economist armed with this essay can say to a country—be it a centrally planned economy or a capitalist economy—that its public policies and private propensities are such that, if not *eventually* changed, dynamical inefficiency is the consequence. But he cannot say that these policies must be changed within the year or in the next billion years. Such wisdom may not be without practical value. But it is to be hoped that some day economists will have stronger recommendations to make in the area of growth policy.

[9] This observation leads to another qualification. In a world of uncertainty, as Pearce (*op. cit.*) has observed, an economy may rationally deepen capital "excessively" in order to possess a "war chest" of capital for consumption in the event of an earthquake, a war, and other probabilistic phenomena. If these events never occur, so that the war chest is never consumed and capital is always "excessive," then, while the war chest strategy will be regretted from hindsight, it cannot be said to be irrational. But I doubt that such uncertainties are of sufficient quantitative importance to justify an appreciable war chest.

The Ramsey Problem
and the Golden Rule
of Accumulation

The purpose of this paper is to describe the use to which the Golden Rule notion can be put in solving the Ramsey problem and to describe the relation that the Golden Rule path bears to the "optimal" growth path in the Ramsey problem. By the "Ramsey problem" I mean the problem of choosing a capital-accumulation program over finite time, given a known social utility function and certain production and consumption constraints. The term is especially descriptive here for I confine myself to a one-sector model and use an additive utility function, as did Frank Ramsey[1] in his path-breaking investigation of the problem nearly forty years ago.

The first part of this paper presents a somewhat informal and slightly simplified version of the original Ramsey model in which the population and technology are constant. In the second part I introduce an exponentially growing population and show how the Golden Rule path has been used to find a solution to the Ramsey problem in this case. The third part introduces exponential labor augmentation (technical progress which is everywhere Harrod neutral) and again uses the Golden Rule path in analyzing the Ramsey problem. This section contains some new results on the conditions for the existence of an optimum when there is no discounting of *individual* utility rates. Some remarks on two difficulties faced by the Ramsey approach to the national saving decision conclude the paper.

[1] F. P. Ramsey, "A Mathematical Theory of Saving," *Economic Journal*, Vol. 38, (December 1928), pp. 543–559.

STATIONARY POPULATION AND TECHNOLOGY

Ramsey postulated a stationary population size for all time. While leisure was one of the variables to be optimized simultaneously with saving in Ramsey's formulation, I shall take per capita leisure to be constant, as most recent analyses do, so that labor at time t, $L(t)$, is proportional to population and therefore constant:

$$L(t) = L_o, \quad L_o > 0. \qquad (1)$$

The technology is also stationary and is summarized by an aggregate production function which makes aggregate output, $Q(t)$, a function of capital, $K(t)$, labor, and possibly other fixed factors:

$$Q(t) = F[K(t), L(t)] \qquad (2)$$

or, since labor is fixed,

$$Q(t) = G[K(t)], \quad G(K) > 0 \text{ for } K > 0. \qquad (3)$$

It is unnecessary to postulate everywhere diminishing marginal productivities or even constant returns to scale. But in the absence of a certain restriction on the utility function to be introduced, it will be necessary to make a capital saturation assumption to be specified shortly.

Supposing for simplicity that there is no depreciation, we can interpret $Q(t)$ as net income. Net income is divided between consumption, $C(t)$, and net investment, $\dot{K}(t) \equiv dK(t)/dt$.

$$C(t) + \dot{K}(t) = Q(t), \quad C(t) \geq 0. \qquad (4)$$

Consumption must be nonnegative.

From (3) and (4), therefore,

$$C(t) + \dot{K}(t) = G[K(t)], \quad C(t) \geq 0. \qquad (5)$$

Also we have the initial condition

$$K(0) = K_o, \quad K_o > 0. \qquad (6)$$

Equations (5) and (6) constitute the production and consumption constraints in the optimization problem.

Turning to the preference side of the model, Ramsey postulated a social utility function of the form

$$U = \int_0^\infty u[C(t)]\, dt, \quad u'(C) > 0, \quad u''(C) < 0 \qquad (7)$$

where u is called the *rate* of (social) utility.

Such a utility function is additive. It follows from work by Gerard Debreu[2], as Tjalling Koopmans[3] has pointed out, that if, in addition to certain postulates guaranteeing that preferences can be represented by some utility function, one postulates "non-complementarity between periods" in the sense that the preferences among consumption paths in any series of periods are independent of what is consumed in other periods, then (and only then) the preferences can be represented by an additive utility function

$$U = u_1(C_1) + u_2(C_2) + \ldots.$$

Further, the utility function *(7)* is "stationary" in the sense that calendar time has no effects on the utility differences associated with different consumption programs. Koopmans indicates that if, in addition to the noncomplementarity postulate, one makes the "stationarity" postulate that preferences among consumption programs beginning next period would be unchanged if these programs were to begin this period, we obtain the utility function

$$U = \sum_{t=1}^\infty \alpha^{t-1} u(C_t), \quad 0 < \alpha < 1,$$

where α is the "discount factor."

Beside the detail that the above function is a sum of discrete utilities rather than an integral, the two functions differ only in that Koopmans discounted future utilities while Ramsey did not, regarding such discounting as "ethically indefensible." Koopmans shows discounting to be a necessary logical consequence of the postulates of his study if one requires the utility function to give

[2] G. Debreu, "Topological Methods in Cardinal Utility Theory," in K. J. Arrow *et al.* (eds.), *Mathematical Methods in the Social Sciences 1959* (Stanford: Stanford University Press, 1960).

[3] T. C. Koopmans, "Stationary Ordinal Utility and Impatience," *Econometrica*, Vol. 28 (April 1960), pp. 287–309.

a complete preference ordering of consumption programs over an infinite time horizon.   (Incidentally, these postulates include a weakened substitute for the noncomplementarity postulate which permits him to derive a utility function with a variable discount factor.) Ramsey's unwillingness to discount presented him with a difficulty from which he sought ingeniously to escape.

Ramsey's objective was the maximization of the social utility function in *(7)* subject to the constraints *(5)* and *(6)*. The difficulty that is immediately encountered is that the postulated technology may permit infinite utility *(U)* to be achieved by more than one feasible consumption program. If there is some sustainable rate of consumption for which the utility rate is positive, i.e., $u[G(K°)] > 0$ for some $K°$ attainable in finite time, then any policy which eventually sustains that consumption rate will cause the utility integral to diverge to plus infinity. When such divergence arises the problem is not determinate.

Nevertheless Ramsey devised a trick to yield a determinate optimization problem. He postulated that either $G(K)$ is bounded from above or that $u(C)$ is bounded from above (or both):

$$G(K) \leq \hat{G} \quad \text{for all } K,$$

or

$$u(C) \leq \bar{u} \quad \text{for all } C.$$

The idea was that on either of these restrictions there would be a maximum sustainable rate of utility— $\hat{u} = u(\hat{C}) = u(\hat{G})$ in the first case, $\bar{u}$ in the second case, the smaller of the two if both $G(K)$ and $u(C)$ are bounded. Ramsey then *minimized* the integral of the *shortfall* of the actual rate of utility, $u(C)$, from the maximum sustainable rate (which he called "bliss"), arguing that there would be at least one feasible consumption program that would make this integral converge and that the optimal consumption program is that program (among those which make the integral converge) which yields the smallest value of the integral.

In fact this restriction is not sufficient for the existence of programs that make the integral converge. If $G(K)$ or $u(C)$ approaches its upper bound asymptotically at too slow a rate, the integral to be minimized will not converge. To simplify matters most contemporary analysts, *e.g.*, Paul Samuelson and

Robert Solow[4], make the overly strong postulate that either $G(K)$ or $u(C)$ can attain its upper bound at a finite K or C, respectively:

$$G(K) = \hat{G}, \; K \geq \hat{K}; \; G'(K) > 0 \text{ for } K < \hat{K}; \qquad (8)$$
$$0 < \hat{K} < \infty;$$

or

$$u(C) = \overline{u}, \; C \geq \overline{C}; \; u'(C) > 0, \; u''(C) < 0 \text{ for } C < \overline{C};$$
$$0 < \overline{C} < \infty.$$

Thus there is capital saturation at $\hat{K}$ or utility satiation at $\overline{C}$, or both. Again, the maximum sustainable rate of utility is $\hat{u} = u(\hat{G})$ or $\overline{u} = u(\overline{C})$ or whichever is smaller if both $\hat{K}$ and $\overline{C}$ exist. In what follows, I suppose that capital saturation is binding, i.e., $\hat{u}$ is the maximum sustainable rate of utility.

Now, with Ramsey, one may minimize the integral of the short-fall of the rate of utility from the bliss rate, $\hat{u}$, or, equivalently, one may maximize, subject to the constraints,

$$V = \int_0^\infty \left(u[C(t)] - \hat{u} \right) dt. \qquad (9)$$

The constant $\hat{u}$ plays the role of a "subtractor" in the integrand.

Supposing always that $K_o < \hat{K}$, meaning that the economy is not initially saturated with capital, there will be many feasible consumption programs which cause the integral in *(9)* to diverge to minus infinity. But since, by saving, it is feasible in finite time to equate $K(t)$ to $\hat{K}$, there must be some programs which cause the integral to converge (to a finite negative number); these are the programs that equate $u[C(t)]$ to $\hat{u}$ in finite time or asymptotically at a sufficiently fast rate. Further, it can be shown that no feasible consumption program can make the integral diverge to plus infinity, or indeed to converge to any positive number. The consumption program which makes the integral converge to the algebraically largest number is designated the "optimal" program, all others giving a smaller V, some of them a V of minus infinity.

[4] P. A. Samuelson and R. M. Solow, "A Complete Capital Model Involving Heterogeneous Capital Goods," *Quarterly Journal of Economics*, Vol. 70, (November 1956), pp. 537–562.

Ramsey and some latter-day writers. have evidently regarded this "optimal" consumption program to be the solution to the *original problem* of maximizing the social utility integral in *(7)*. But the maximization of V in *(9)* is a different problem from maximizing U in *(7)*. As was seen earlier, U fails to discriminate among a certain class of consumption programs that V does discriminate among; and V fails to discriminate among some consumption programs that U discriminates among. More formally, V is not a monotonically increasing function of U, since it is possible for U to be undefined where V is defined and conversely, so that the two problems are not equivalent.

This does not imply that the solution to the V maximization problem cannot be regarded as "optimal." But a new criterion of optimality is required.

The modern approach to the divergence problem, which may be found in work of Christian von Weizsäcker[5], H. Atsumi[6], and somewhat implicitly in work by Koopmans[7], is the following. A consumption program (over infinite time), $C_1(t)$, is said to be preferred or indifferent to another consumption program, $C_2(t)$, if there exists a $T°$ such that for all $T \geq T°$

$$\int_0^T u[C_1(t)] \, dt \geq \int_0^T u[C_2(t)] \, dt$$

$C_1(t)$ is strictly preferred if the strict inequality holds. This has been called the "overtaking principle."

A feasible consumption program $C^*(t)$ is said to be optimal if for every other feasible consumption program $C(t)$, $C(t) \neq C^*(t)$ for some t, there exists a $T°$ (not necessarily the same for each

[5] C. C. von Weizsäcker, "Existence of Optimal Programs of Accumulation for an Infinite Time Horizon," *Review of Economic Studies*, Vol. 32, (April 1965), pp. 85–104.

[6] H. Atsumi, "Neoclassical Growth and the Efficient Program of Capital Accumulation," *Review of Economic Studies*, Vol. 32 (April 1965), pp. 127–136.

[7] T. C. Koopmans, "On the Concept of Optimal Economic Growth," in *Le Rôle de L'analyse Econometrique dans la Formulation de Plans de Développement*, Vol. 28, Part 1 in the series *Scripta Varia* (Pontificia Academia Scientarium, Vatican City, 1965), pp. 225–287.

alternative program) such that for all $T \geq T^\circ$

$$\int_0^T u[C^*(t)] \, dt \geq \int_0^T u[C(t)] \, dt.$$

The optimum is unique if there exists a T° such that the strict inequality holds.

No discounting of future utility rates is necessary here (although one could introduce utility discounting). The price paid for this luxury is that the proposed preference criterion may fail to order many pairs of feasible consumption programs. Consider a pair of consumption programs $C_0(t)$ and $C_1(t)$ and a sequence of values $T_1, T_2, \ldots$ converging to plus infinity such that

$$\int_0^{T_i} u[C_0(t)] < \int_0^{T_i} u[C_1(t)] \, dt, \quad i = 1, 2, \ldots$$

Then $C_0(t)$ is *not* preferred or indifferent to $C_1(t)$. But for the same pair of consumption programs there may exist a different sequence of values $T'_1, T'_2, \ldots$ converging to plus infinity such that

$$\int_0^{T'_i} u[C_1(t)] \, dt < \int_0^{T'_i} u[C_0(t)] \, dt, \quad i = 1, 2, \ldots$$

Then $C_1(t)$ is *not* preferred or indifferent to $C_0(t)$. Since neither program is preferred or indifferent to the other on the proposed criterion, the criterion fails to give a preference ordering of such pairs of consumption programs. If discounting were introduced, one could order all programs by comparing the limits of the integrals as $T \to \infty$.

This weakness in the preference criterion is of no importance if there exists an optimal program in the above sense. However, no optimum need exist. *Case 1:* No optimum exists if for every feasible consumption program $C_1(t)$ there exists a feasible consumption program $C_2(t)$ and some T° such that for all $T \geq T^\circ$

$$\int_0^T u[C_1(t)] \, dt < \int_0^T u[C_2(t)] \, dt.$$

In this case, there being no best feasible program, the optimization problem is insoluble. *Case 2:* No optimum (in the above sense) exists if there is a class of consumption programs for which no preference ordering is given (as with the pair $C_0(t)$ and $C_1(t)$ discussed earlier) all of which are preferred or indifferent to all programs outside this class. Then the programs in this class are "good"—there is no better path—but there exists no optimal path in the sense of the present criterion. Nevertheless, if there are certain restrictions on the technology (or on $u(C)$) such as were made above, an optimum in this sense will exist.

This optimality criterion justifies Ramsey's identification of the V-maximizing consumption policy as the optimal consumption policy. For if there exists a consumption path $\widetilde{C}(t)$ (which is feasible for *some* initial K, not necessarily the given K_o) and hence some corresponding path of the rate of utility $u[\widetilde{C}(t)]$ such that maximization of

$$\int_0^\infty \left(u[C(t)] - u[\widetilde{C}(t)] \right) dt$$

yields a solution, say $C^{**}(t)$, then $C^{**}(t)$ is an optimal path $C^*(t)$ in the sense of the new optimality criterion. If the maximum is unique, the optimum is also unique.[8] In the Ramsey model, the path $C(t) = \hat{C} = G(\hat{K})$ is the path $\widetilde{C}(t)$ and $\hat{u} = u(\hat{C})$ is the subtractor, $u[\widetilde{C}(t)]$. Thus we have described the modern basis for Ramsey's trick of maximizing V instead of U.

When Ramsey maximized *(9)* subject to the constraints *(5)* and *(6)* (given the existence of a $\hat{K}$) he obtained the following remarkably simple formula for the optimal saving policy:

$$\dot{K} = \frac{\hat{u} - u(C)}{u'(C)}. \qquad (10)$$

[8] If $C^{**}(t)$ is a unique maximizing path, then

$$\int_0^\infty [u(C^{**}) - u(\widetilde{C})]\, dt > \int_0^\infty [u(C) - u(\widetilde{C})]\, dt$$

for all other C paths, $C \neq C^{**}$ for some t. Then

$$\int_0^\infty [u(C^{**}) - u(\widetilde{C})]\, dt - \int_0^\infty [u(C) - u(\widetilde{C})]\, dt > 0$$

and hence

$$\int_0^\infty [u(C^{**}) - u(C)]\, dt > 0.$$

If the following integrals are continuous in T, it follows that, for some T^o,

$$\int_0^T u(C^{**})\, dt > \int_0^T u(C)\, dt, \quad T \geq T^o,$$

so that $C^{**}(t)$ is the unique optimum.

Before discussing some features of this solution, we shall present two methods by which it can be derived.

Ramsey reported that Keynes produced an ingenious proof of this formula using the following argument. (See Ramsey's statement of the argument or James Meade's more detailed presentation.[9]) Suppose that it is decided to do an extra "day's worth" of saving. Then the whole time schedule of progress towards "bliss" will be advanced by one day (if the economy reverts to its previous consumption policy after today). Therefore there will be a gain of one extra day at bliss,[10] hence a gain of $\hat{u}$. But the utility, u, that would have been enjoyed tomorrow will be forever lost (since it is the utility rate that would otherwise have been enjoyed on the following day that is enjoyed tomorrow). Hence the true gain from advancing the schedule is $\hat{u} - u$. The cost of doing so is the extra saving multiplied by the marginal utility of consumption, so that if S is the amount that was being saved per day the cost is $Su'(C)$. Now if the original consumption program was optimal there will be no gain or loss from departing (infinitesimally) from the original program, so that $Su'(C) = \hat{u} - u$, which is *(10)*. (Of course, these formulas for the cost and gain are only approximations in the discrete-time context of Keynes's argument but it is possible to formulate a somewhat analogous argument in continuous time.)

There are a variety of more formal derivations of the Ramsey result. We choose here to use the technique of dynamic programming developed by Richard Bellman.[11]

First, we define $w(K_o)$ to be the maximum value of V when the initial stock of capital is K_o. That is,

$$w(K_o) = \max \int_0^\infty \left(u[C(t)] - \hat{u} \right) dt$$

subject to $C(t) + \dot{K}(t) = G(K)$.

$$K(0) = K_o$$

(11)

---

[9] J. E. Meade, *Trade and Welfare*: Mathematical Supplement (London: Oxford University Press, 1955).

[10] Actually, bliss is approached only asymptotically which indicates that Keynes's argument requires some modification to be valid.

[11] R. E. Bellman, *Dynamic Programming* (Princeton: Princeton University Press, 1957), pp. 249–250.

Now Bellman's "principle of optimality" states that whatever the initial state and initial policy, the remaining decisions must be optimal with regard to the state resulting from the first decision if the over-all policy is to be optimal. The approach is to divide time into an initial small interval of length Δ, over which the initial policy is to be made, and the remaining open-ended interval beginning at $t = \Delta$, over which it is assumed that an optimal policy is followed. If the average rate of consumption over the initial interval is C then the amount of utility (V) earned is approximately $[u(C) - \hat{u}]\Delta$ and the capital stock at $t = \Delta$ will be approximately $K(\Delta) = K_o + \Delta[G(K_o) - C]$. Hence we obtain the following approximate relation

$$w(K_o) = \max_C \{[u(C) - \hat{u}]\Delta + w(K_o + \Delta[G(K_o) - C])\}. \quad (12)$$

Using an approximation for $w(K_o + \Delta[G(K_o) - C])$ gives

$$\begin{aligned} w(K_o) = \max_C \{&[u(C) - \hat{u}]\Delta + w(K_o) \\ &+ w'(K_o)\Delta[G(K_o) - C]\}. \end{aligned} \quad (13)$$

Subtracting the constant $w(K_o)$ from both sides then gives

$$0 = \max_C \{[u(C) - \hat{u}]\Delta + w'(K_o)\Delta[G(K_o) - C]\}. \quad (14)$$

Dividing by Δ and letting $\Delta \to 0$ yields

$$0 = \max_C \{u(C) - \hat{u} + w'(K_o)[G(K_o) - C]\} \quad (15)$$

where now C represents the initial rate of consumption.

From *(15)* we see that if C is optimal, so that the expression in braces is maximized, then we have the following equation in the optimal C:

$$u(C) - \hat{u} + w'(K_o)[G(K_o) - C] = 0. \quad (16)$$

Further, if the maximum is an interior one, then the derivative with respect to C of the expression in braces in *(15)* must equal zero, which yields another equation in optimal C:

$$u'(C) - w'(K_o) = 0. \quad (17)$$

From *(16)* and *(17)* we obtain

$$G(K_o) - C = \frac{\hat{u} - u(C)}{u'(C)} \qquad (18)$$

which is *(10)*, the Ramsey-Keynes formula.

Some features of Ramsey's solution can be brought out by the geometric representation of the formula in Figure 4. To obtain

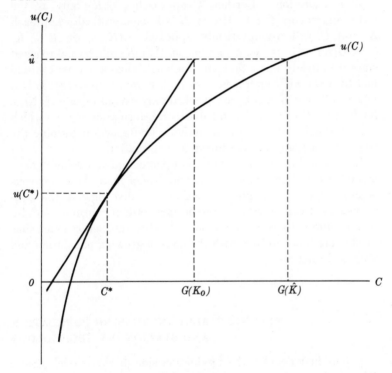

the optimal rate of consumption one needs to know only initial income, $G(K_o)$, the shape of the function $u(C)$ and $\hat{u}$. Hence variations of the production function which leave initial income and $\hat{u}$ unchanged have no effect upon the optimal rate of consumption; in a sense, therefore, C^* is independent of the marginal product of capital and the functional distribution of income. Further the optimal policy is "myopic" in the special sense that the present value of future income or other wealthlike variables play no part. This rather simple dependence of optimal consumption on income alone, given $u(C)$ and $\hat{u}$, may have suggested to Keynes the consumption function of the *General Theory*. (The optimal marginal propensity to consume in Ramsey's model is positive but it need not be less than unity as Keynes postulated.)

The diagram shows that if $K_o < \hat{K}$, then $C < G(K_o)$ so that $\dot{K} > 0$; thus there is saving as long as the economy is short of capital saturation. Further, C approaches $G(K)$ only as the latter approaches $G(\hat{K})$. Hence, K will asymptotically approach $\hat{K}$ and C will asymptotically approach $G(\hat{K})$. At $K = \hat{K}$, $C = G(\hat{K})$. (It is not a new result that $\hat{K}$ will be approached since we already knew that all programs "eligible" to be optimal had to make $u(C)$ approach $\hat{u}$ so that V would converge; it is a new result that $\hat{K}$ will be approached only asymptotically.) Note finally that $\dot{K}$ is invariant to a linear transformation of $u(C)$ which is as it should be since the underlying preferences determine the function $u(C)$ only up to a linear transformation.

In closing this section we note that Samuelson and Solow[12] have extended the Ramsey analysis to the case of many heterogeneous capital goods. The present author has investigated the consequences of capital risk for the optimal rate of consumption also in an infinite time-horizon model.[13] But the major extensions needed are those to cope with the facts of growing population and technical progress.

EXPONENTIALLY INCREASING POPULATION
AND STATIONARY TECHNOLOGY

Let us first develop the production side of this model. Since labor is increasing exponentially, the counterpart of *(1)* in the previous model is

$$L(t) = L_o e^{\gamma t}, \quad \gamma > 0. \tag{19}$$

[12] Samuelson and Solow, *op. cit.*

[13] E. S. Phelps, "The Accumulation of Risky Capital," *Econometrica*, Vol. 30, (October 1962), pp. 729–743.

The technology is still supposed to be stationary so that the production function is independent of time:

$$Q(t) = F[K(t), L(t)]. \qquad (20)$$

Now, however, we posit constant return to scale, twice differentiability, diminishing marginal productivities, and that both factors are essential to production, so that one may write

$$Q(t) = L(t)f(k(t)) \qquad (21)$$

where

$$k(t) = \frac{K(t)}{L(t)}, \ f(k(t)) = F[k(t), 1],$$

and

$$f(0) = 0, \ f'(k) > 0, \ f''(k) < 0, \ f'(\infty) = 0.$$

Again supposing there is no depreciation, we have that consumption per unit labor, c, (which is proportional to consumption per head since we are fixing leisure per head) and investment per unit labor sum to output per unit labor:

$$c(t) + \frac{\dot{K}(t)}{L(t)} = f(k(t)), \ \ c(t) \geq 0, \qquad (22)$$

where

$$c(t) = \frac{C(t)}{L(t)}.$$

Since

$$\frac{\dot{k}}{k} = \frac{\dot{K}}{K} - \frac{\dot{L}}{L}$$

$$\dot{k} = \frac{\dot{K}}{L} - \gamma k$$

we therefore have

$$c(t) + \dot{k}(t) = g(k(t)), \ \ c(t) \geq 0 \qquad (23)$$

where

$$g(k(t)) = f(k(t)) - \gamma k(t).$$

Finally we have the initial condition

$$k(0) = k_o, \ \ k_o > 0. \qquad (24)$$

Equations *(23)* and *(24)* constitute the constraints in the present problem; they are analogous to *(5)* and *(6)* in the previous problem. The equations are identical but for the fact that *(23)* and *(24)* are in *per capita* terms and that, as we shall see, $g(k)$ is somewhat different from $G(K)$. I shall later place restrictions on $f(k)$ such that $g(k)$ reaches a maximum at some finite $\hat{k}$, as we supposed $G(K)$ to do. But I first consider the preference side of the model.

In specifying our criterion of optimality I wish to be unspecific about the form of the Ramsey-like utility integral. Let us therefore write $u = u[c(t), t]$ which is as general as one can be with respect to the dependence of u on consumption, population (which is an exogenously given function of time), and time. Then we say that a feasible consumption program $c^*(t)$ is optimal if and only if for every other feasible path $c(t)$, $c(t) \neq c^*(t)$ for some t, there exists a $T°$ such that for all $T \geq T°$

$$\int_0^T u[c^*(t), t]\, dt \geq \int_0^T u[c(t), t]\, dt.$$

Now to the matter of preferences. Pearce,[14] Srinivasan,[15] Uzawa,[16] Koopmans,[17] von Weizsäcker,[18] Inagaki,[19] Atsumi,[20] Samuelson,[21] Cass,[22] and others have produced a variety of utility functions for consideration in solving the present problem and related problems. Probably the single most popular function, used extensively (though not exclusively) by Koopmans and von Weizsäcker, is the one which makes the rate of social utility, u,

[14] I. F. Pearce, "The End of the Golden Age in Solovia," *American Economic Review*, Vol. 52 (December 1962), pp. 1088–1097.

[15] T. N. Srinivasan, "Optimal Savings in a Two-Sector Model of Growth," *Econometrica*, Vol. 32 (July 1964), pp. 358–373.

[16] H. Uzawa, "Optimal Growth in a Two-Sector Model," *Review of Economic Studies*, Vol. 31 (January 1964), pp. 1–24.

[17] Koopmans, *op. cit.*

[18] Weizsäcker, *op. cit.*

[19] M. Inagaki, "The Golden Utility Path," Memorandum, Netherlands Economic Institute, Rotterdam (November 1963).

[20] Atsumi, *op. cit.*

[21] P. A. Samuelson, "A Catenary Turnpike Theorem Involving Consumption and the Golden Rule," *American Economic Review*, Vol. 51 (June 1965), pp. 486–496.

[22] D. Cass, "Optimum Growth in an Aggregative Model of Capital Accumulation," *Review of Economic Studies*, Vol. 32 (July 1965), pp. 233–240.

an increasing, concave, and unbounded function only of *per capita* consumption; that is,

$$U(T) = \int_0^T u[c(t)] \, dt, \; u'(c) > 0, \; u''(c) < 0, \quad (25)$$

gives the social utility accumulated up to $t = T$ of a path $c(t)$. The quantity $u(c(t))$ is sometimes called the rate of *per capita* utility; I shall simply designate it as the rate of utility.

It is sometimes said that a utility function like *(25)* involves no "discounting" of future "utilities." But this is somewhat misleading for as Koopmans has pointed out, while *(25)* treats "generations" alike (to make somewhat figurative use of the term "generation"), it does not treat "individuals" alike (again somewhat figuratively). Suppose, in calculating social utility at $t = T$, $U(T)$, one integrated over the sum of the social utility rates assigned to the living individuals at each moment of time. Then, if $v_i[c_i(t), t]$ denoted the individual social utility rate of the ith individual and $c_i(t)$ his consumption rate at time t, one would have

$$U(T) = \int_0^T \sum_{i=1}^{L(t)} v_i[c_i(t), t] \, dt$$

where $L(t)$ (an integer) is the size of the population at t. Now if, at every t, consumption is equalized and the individual social utility-rate functions are identical, so that $v_i[c_i(t), t] = v[c(t), t]$, then, treating population size as a continuous variable given by *(19)*, one would have (letting $L_o = 1$)

$$U(T) = \int_0^T e^{\gamma t} v[c(t), t] \, dt.$$

Now if "equal treatment of individuals" demands, as Koopmans suggests, that we do not "discount" individual social utility rates, so that $v[c(t), t]$ is, say, $u[c(t)]$, then our social utility integral would be of the form

$$U(T) = \int_0^T e^{\gamma t} u[c(t)] \, dt$$

which differs from the proposed *(25)*. It becomes clear, therefore, that *(25)* can be interpreted as *discounting individual utility rates* by the population growth rate γ:

$$U(T) = \int_0^T e^{\gamma t} v[c(t), t]\, dt = \int_0^T e^{\gamma t}(e^{-\gamma t} u[c(t)])\, dt$$

$$= \int_0^T u[c(t)]\, dt.$$

While I shall later consider the implications of postulating the equal-treatment-of-individuals function, let us return to *(25)* and examine the Koopmans-von Weizsäcker-Atsumi method of solution. (Srinivasan, Uzawa, and Cass use a different utility function, and, correspondingly, a different approach.)

If one attempts to maximize the limit of $U(T)$ in *(25)* as T goes to infinity, subject to the constraints *(23)* and *(24)*, one may encounter, as did Ramsey in the stationary population problem, the difficulty that more than one feasible consumption program will cause the integral to diverge. The problem will arise if there are sustainable rates of *per capita* consumption for which $u(c) > 0$. To overcome this difficulty the three aforementioned writers employ a trick analogous to Ramsey's trick in the same difficulty: they use the Golden Rule notion to establish the existence of a maximum sustainable rate of utility, $\hat{u}$, which can be introduced to make convergent the limit of the utility integral.

Suppose that $f'(0) > \gamma$, hence $g'(0) > 0$. Since $f'(\infty) = 0$ (labor required for production) and $f''(k) < 0$ (diminishing returns), the function $g(k)$ will then achieve a unique maximum, $\hat{c} > 0$, at some $\hat{k} > 0$:

$$g'(\hat{k}) = 0 \text{ or } f'(\hat{k}) = \gamma, \quad \hat{k} > 0$$
$$\hat{c} = g(\hat{k}) > 0, \quad \hat{u} = u(\hat{c}). \tag{26}$$

$\hat{c}$ is the maximum sustainable rate of *per capita* consumption and $\hat{u}$ is the maximum sustainable rate of utility. The path, $k(t) = \hat{k}$, is, of course, the Golden Rule path; it is the consumption-maximizing golden-age path. On this path, the marginal product of capital, $f'(k)$, equals the population-growth rate and investment equals competitive profits. Thus our postulates imply that a Golden Rule path exists. The next step is to assign to the Golden Rule path the same role played by the capital-saturation path in the stationary population model. The utility rate corresponding to the Golden Rule path, $\hat{u}$, is subtracted from the actual rate of utility, $u(c(t))$, to form the new integral

$$V = \int_0^\infty \left(u[c(t)] - \hat{u} \right) dt \qquad (27)$$

analogous to *(9)*.

Once again, if there exists a feasible path which maximizes V, this is an optimal path in the sense of the above optimality criterion; if the maximum is unique, so is the optimum. Koopmans shows that a unique maximum exists. In particular, there is no divergence problem: V is bounded from above for all feasible consumption paths and all initial capital stocks. If the economy starts below the Golden Rule path, $k_o < \hat{k}$, the integral is negative for all feasible paths; but since the Golden Rule path can be reached in finite time, there are necessarily some paths which cause the integral to converge (to a finite negative number). If the economy starts above the Golden Rule path, the integral, while positive, will still converge (for all paths of interest). Thus there are no paths which are "infinitely better" than the Golden Rule path.

Since the problem of maximizing *(27)* subject to *(23)* and *(24)* is mathematically identical, in every essential respect, to the previous problem of maximizing *(9)* subject to *(5)* and *(6)*, one necessarily obtains for the optimal rate of consumption per head the Ramsey-like formula

$$\dot{k} = \frac{\hat{u} - u(c)}{u'(c)} . \qquad (28)$$

Recalling that $\dot{k} = \dot{K}/L - \gamma k$, one can write *(28)* in the form

$$\dot{K} = \left[\frac{\hat{u} - u(c)}{u'(c)} + \gamma k \right] L_o e^{\gamma t}. \qquad (28a)$$

Setting $L_o = 1$ (which we are free to do), we see that *(28a)* gives *(10)* of the previous model if and only if $\gamma = 0$ (since, if $L_o e^{\gamma t} = 1$, the C of the previous model is equal to consumption per head, c, of the present model).

The features of this solution are, of course, the same as in the previous model. If $k_o = \hat{k}$, we have $c = g(\hat{k})$, $\dot{k} = 0$ and the

Golden Rule path will be followed. If $k_o < \hat{k}$, we have $c < g(k)$ for all t and $k(t)$ will approach $\hat{k}$ asymptotically and monotonically. Likewise, if $k_o > \hat{k}$, $c > g(k)$ for all t and $\hat{k}$ will be approached asymptotically and monotonically.

A question that may occur to many readers is: how, if at all, does the optimal rate of consumption depend upon the population growth rate? We note first that in the long run, $\dot{K} \to \gamma \hat{k} e^{\gamma t} > 0$ if $\gamma > 0$ (setting $L_o = 1$) while $\dot{K} \to 0$ if $\gamma = 0$ and a finite $\hat{K}$ exists (which means in the present context that $\hat{k}$ does not go to infinity as γ goes to zero), so that, in the long run, there is more saving when there is population growth, both absolutely and as a ratio to income. Since income per head will, of course, be smaller in the long run when there is population growth (there being less capital per head asymptotically), consumption per head will also be smaller in the long run.

As for *initial* saving, given income per head $G(K_o) = f(k_o)$, and labor force $L_o = 1$, there are two conflicting influences: on the one hand, the greater γ, the smaller will be $g(k_o)$, the amount available to be divided between consumption per head and the increase of capital per head, and this decreases optimal consumption per head as manipulation of a diagram like Figure 4 will show; on the other hand, the greater γ, the smaller will be $\hat{k}$, $\hat{c}$, and hence $\hat{u}$ and this increases the optimal consumption per head as diagrammatics will easily show. As for global comparisons of the sort $\gamma = 0$ vs. $\gamma > 0$, it is pretty clear that one can devise g and u functions that will make the former or the latter effect decisive, whichever is desired. It might be of interest, however, to verify that the derivative $dc/d\gamma$ is of indeterminate sign without new restrictions on $g(k)$ and $u(c)$. First, write *(28)* in the following form to obtain initially optimal consumption per head, c_o:

$$[g(k_o) - c_o]u'(c_o) = u[g(\hat{k})] - u(c_o). \qquad (28b)$$

Taking the total differential we have

$$u'(c_o) \frac{dg(k_o)}{d\gamma} d\gamma + \{-u'(c_o) + u''(c_o)[g(k_o) - c_o]\} dc_o$$
$$= u'[g(\hat{k})] \frac{dg(\hat{k})}{d\gamma} d\gamma - u'(c_o) dc_o, \qquad (29)$$

where

$$\frac{dg(k_o)}{d\gamma} = -k_o, \quad \frac{dg(\hat{k})}{d\gamma} = -\hat{k}.$$

Hence

$$\frac{dc_o}{d\gamma} = \frac{u'(c_o)k_o - u'[g(\hat{k})]\hat{k}}{u''(c_o)[g(k_o) - c_o]}. \quad (30)$$

While the denominator is unambiguously negative, the numerator may be of either sign. The first term there (taken as a ratio to the denominator) represents the first aforementioned influence of γ on c through its effect upon $g(k_o)$ (which influence is negative as we indicated earlier), while the second term represents the second influence of γ on c through its effect upon $g(\hat{k})$ and hence $\hat{u}$ (which influence is positive). Curiously, if $k_o = \hat{k}$, so that initial $c_o = g(\hat{k})$, then $dc_o/d\gamma = 0$ (initially) but there is otherwise no presumption of such invariance. (This last result does *not* mean that Golden Rule $\hat{c}$ is invariant to γ; in fact, $dg(\hat{k})/d\gamma < 0$.)

In this connection I note finally that if there were "utility satiation" at some $\bar{c}$ for which $\bar{c} < \hat{c}$ then $\bar{u} = u(\bar{c})$ would take the place of $\hat{u}$ in *(28)* and, since $\bar{u}$ would presumably be invariant to γ, the second of our two influences would be absent so that an increase of γ would unambiguously decrease optimal consumption.

As we have seen, the optimal accumulation policy drives the economy toward the Golden Rule path and hence drives the marginal product of capital or real interest rate toward the population growth rate. It may seem puzzling to some readers that the economy should stop at the Golden Rule path. Should not society deepen capital further as long as the interest rate exceeds the rate of pure time preference (the utility discount rate) which has been taken to be zero? There are a number of answers to this question. First, an accumulation policy which permanently drove the interest rate finitely below the population growth rate could not be optimal since growth paths which violate the Golden Rule in this manner are dynamically inefficient. Second, as we saw earlier, there is in reality implicit discounting of *individual* utility rates at the rate γ so it should perhaps be expected that capital deepening would cease as the interest rate approached the population growth rate. However, the following heuristic exercise may make the "optimality" of the Golden Rule path especially clear.

Consider the discrete-time analogue of our present model and suppose that society contemplates a departure from the path it originally intended to follow: $c_0, c_1, \ldots$. In particular suppose that the L_o people in period zero each save an extra unit in period zero with the intention of consuming the extra capital plus the interest on it in period one, thus permitting $c_2, c_3, \ldots$ to be unchanged. The initial loss of utility will be $u'(c_0)$ since consumption per head has fallen by one unit. The increase in *total* consumption next period will be $L_o(1 + r)$ where r is the rate of interest or marginal product of capital. If the number of people next period, L_1, is equal to $(1 + \gamma)L_o$ then the increase in consumption *per head* in period one will be only $(1 + r)(1 + \gamma)^{-1}$ and hence the gain in utility will be only $(1 + r)(1 + \gamma)^{-1}u'(c_1)$. Now if the original path is optimal, the net gain from such proposed alterations will be approximately zero; hence, for every t,

$$u'(c_t) = (1 + r_t)(1 + \gamma)^{-1}u'(c_{t+1}). \qquad (31)$$

We see that a stationary program, $c_0 = c_1 = c_2 = \ldots, r_t = r$, will satisfy this necessary optimality condition only if $u'(c) = 0$, which the assumption of an unbounded utility function excludes, or if $r = \gamma$, which is the Golden Rule path. And if $r = \gamma$ initially, the stationary program $c_1 = c_2 = \ldots = \hat{c}$, that is, obedience to the Golden Rule, will satisfy this condition and hence be optimal.

Equation *(31)* is the discrete-time version of the necessary Euler condition for a maximum V in *(27)* subject to *(23)* and *(24)*:

$$\left[\frac{d}{dt} u'(c)\right] \Big/ u'(c) = -(r - \gamma), \quad r = f'(k). \qquad (32)$$

This equation tells the same story as *(31)*.

David Cass[23] and Koopmans [24] have also studied the Ramsey problem (with $\gamma \geq 0$) when future utility rates are discounted at a positive rate ρ. Then the problem is one of maximizing

$$U = \int_0^\infty e^{-\rho t}u[c(t)]\, dt, \quad \rho > 0, \qquad (33)$$

[23] Cass, *op. cit.*
[24] Koopmans, *op. cit.*

subject to *(23)* and *(24)*. While ρ is called the discount rate, we should remember that $\rho + \gamma$ is implicitly the rate at which *individual* utility rates are being discounted. Cass and Koopmans postulate, as usual, that $u'(c) > 0$, $u''(c) < 0$ and $u(c)$ unbounded. Note that since $\rho > 0$, the utility integral will necessarily converge (by virtue of the concavity of u and f), so there is no need for the Golden Rule device. (It should be mentioned that T. N. Srinivasan[25] and Hirofumi Uzawa[26] had earlier studied a similar problem, where $u(c) = c$, in a *two*-sector model. The results in these two papers resemble those obtained in the one-sector model considered here. See also the multisector analysis by Roy Radner,[27] especially of the "linear logarithmic" case.)

In this new problem, the analogue of *(31)* is

$$u'(c_t) = (1 + r_t)(1 + \gamma)^{-1}(1 + \rho)^{-1}u'(c_{t+1}) \qquad (34)$$

if one replaces $e^{-\rho t}$ by $(1 + \rho)^{-t}$. The Euler equation is now

$$\left[\frac{d}{dt}\,u'(c)\right]\Big/ u'(c) = -(r - \gamma - \rho). \qquad (35)$$

Like *(32)*, this states that the proportionate rate of decrease of the discounted marginal utility of per capita consumption, in this case $(du'/dt)/u' - \rho$, must equal the excess of the rate of interest over the population growth rate.

These two equations indicate that, since $u'(c) > 0$ for all c, the only stationary equilibrium that can be optimal is that path on which $r = \rho + \gamma$. If initially $r = \rho + \gamma$, a stationary path with constant per capita consumption and constant r will satisfy the Euler equation. Such a path is (like the Golden Rule path) a particular golden-age path. Following Inagaki,[28] I shall call this path the Golden Utility path. Clearly it coincides with the Golden Rule path if and only if $\rho = 0$; if $\rho > 0$, the Golden Utility path gives a lower capital intensity, k, lower income per head and, of course, smaller consumption per head.

[25] Srinivasan, *op. cit.*

[26] Uzawa, *op. cit.*

[27] R. Radner, *Notes on the Theory of Economic Planning*, (Athens: Center of Economic Research, 1963) and "Optimal Growth in a Linear-Logarithmic Economy," *International Economic Review*, Vol. 7 (January 1966), pp. 1–33.

[28] Inagaki, *op. cit.*

Cass and Koopmans have shown that if the economy starts from a position off the Golden Utility path, the latter will be approached asymptotically and monotonically. When $\gamma = 0$, this coincides with Ramsey's result that if there is a constant pure time preference rate, $\rho > 0$, the rate of interest will approach that rate asymptotically.

It might be thought that if $\rho < 0$ there still exists a Golden Utility path with $r = \rho + \gamma < \gamma$ but this is not so. Such a stationary path satisfies the necessary Euler condition but that path, and any path asymptotic to it, cannot be optimal in the sense of our optimality criterion for it is dynamically inefficient (i.e., dominated by another path). In fact, as Koopmans has shown, there is no optimal consumption program when $\rho < 0$.

First, we recall, letting $\sigma \equiv -\rho > 0$, that an optimum exists if and only if there is at least one feasible path, $c^*(t)$, and some T^o such that, for every other feasible path $c_o(t)$, $c_o(t) \neq c^*(t)$ for some t,

$$\int_0^T e^{\sigma t} u[c^*(t)] \, dt \geq \int_0^T e^{\sigma t} u[c_o(t)] \, dt \quad \text{for all } T \geq T^o.$$

Hence, if an optimum exists (for the given k_o), there must be a path $\tilde{c}(t)$ and some T^o such that for every other feasible path $c(t)$, $c(t) \neq \tilde{c}(t)$,

$$W(T) = \int_0^T e^{\sigma t} (u[c(t)] - u[\tilde{c}(t)]) \, dt \leq 0, \quad \text{for all } T \geq T^o.$$

In particular, any optimal path, $c^*(t)$, is such a path (i.e., will fill the role of $\tilde{c}(t)$.)

Now Koopmans proved that if $\rho < 0$, i.e., $\sigma > 0$, then for every feasible $\tilde{c}(t)$ path and every number $N > 0$ there exists another feasible path $c(t)$ and a number T^o such that[29]

$$W(T) > N \quad \text{for all } T \geq T^o.$$

Hence there exists no optimum when $\rho < 0$.

The intuitive explanation offered by Koopmans is that if we start on the Golden Rule path, where $u'(c) = u'(\hat{c})$ for all t, then a sacrifice of one unit of *per capita* consumption in any short

[29] The proof is overly strong since $N = 0$ would be sufficient.

initial interval Δ will permit an equal gain of *per capita* consumption in any subsequent interval of equal duration; the utility initially sacrificed will be $u'(\hat{c}) \, \Delta$ and the utility gained will be $e^{\sigma t}u'(\hat{c}) \, \Delta$ which is greater than the sacrifice if $\sigma > 0$. But it will always pay to delay indefinitely the date t at which the fruit of the initial sacrifice is reaped, which suggests that there is no optimum. (The example certainly shows that the Golden Rule path is not optimal, as does the Euler equation *(35)* when $\rho \neq 0$.)

To close this part of the essay, we briefly mention another result which is really somewhat out of the present context. Suppose that all the equations on the production side, *(19)* to *(24)*, continue to apply but that the world is expected with certainty to come to an end at some $t = T$, or at least that only the period, $0 \leq t \leq T$, is of interest. A terminal capital constraint of the form $k(T) \geq k_T \geq 0$ is stipulated.

Samuelson[30] and Cass[31] then investigated the optimal accumulation program in the interval $[0, T]$. Samuelson, working with a utility function like *(25)*,

$$U(T) = \int_0^T u[c(t)] \, dt, \qquad (36)$$

showed that the optimal $k(t)$ path would "arch" (in catenary fashion) toward the Golden Rule path, $\hat{k}$, and that, as T becomes sufficiently large, the optimal path $k(t)$ will spend an arbitrarily large proportion of the time arbitrarily near the Golden Rule path. Thus, the Golden Rule path is a kind of "turnpike" quite similar to the von Neumann ray in models of a different character. (See the references given by Samuelson for the literature on the Turnpike Theorem.) Most of the time the rate of interest, r, will be close to γ, its Golden Rule value.

Cass, working with the more general utility function

$$U(T) = \int_0^T e^{-\rho t}u[c(t)] \, dt, \quad \rho \geq -\gamma, \qquad (37)$$

showed that the path on which $r = \rho + \gamma \geq 0$ possesses the identical turnpike property.

[30] Samuelson, *op. cit.*
[31] D. Cass, *Studies in the Theory of Optimum Economic Growth*, (Ph.D. Dissertation, Stanford University, 1965).

TECHNICAL PROGRESS AND EXPONENTIAL
POPULATION GROWTH

I first develop the production side of a dynamic economy in which population grows exponentially or is constant, technical progress is labor augmenting, and the rate of labor augmentation is constant for all time.

The rate of growth of population and labor, γ, is nonnegative and constant:

$$L(t) = L_o e^{\gamma t}, \quad \gamma \geq 0. \qquad (38)$$

The production function differs from *(20)* only in that there is a constant rate of labor augmentation, λ:

$$Q(t) = F[K(t), e^{\lambda t}L(t)] \qquad (39)$$

whence, if we continue to denote by $k(t)$ the capital-labor ratio (*not* the capital-augmented labor ratio as it is so frequently convenient to do),

$$Q(t) = e^{\lambda t}L(t)f\left[\frac{k(t)}{e^{\lambda t}}\right] = e^{\lambda t}L(t)f[e^{-\lambda t}k(t)] \qquad (40)$$

where

$$k(t) = \frac{K(t)}{L(t)}, \ f\left[\frac{k(t)}{e^{\lambda t}}\right] = F\left[\frac{k(t)}{e^{\lambda t}}, 1\right]$$

and

$$f(0) = 0, \ f'(k) > 0, \ f''(k) < 0, \ f'(\infty) = 0.$$

Since consumption plus investment equal output, we have

$$c(t) + \frac{\dot{K}(t)}{L(t)} = e^{\lambda t}f[e^{-\lambda t}k(t)] \qquad (41)$$

where

$$c(t) = \frac{C(t)}{L(t)}.$$

Since $\dot{k} = \dot{K}/L - \gamma k$, we therefore have

$$c(t) + \dot{k}(t) = e^{\lambda t}f[e^{-\lambda t}k(t)] - \gamma k(t), \ c(t) \geq 0. \qquad (42)$$

In any golden age, $c(t)$, $k(t)$, and hence $\dot{k}(t)$ grow like $e^{\lambda t}$. Noting this, it can easily be shown, using *(42)*, that on the (interior) Golden Rule path (if it exists), $k(t) = \hat{k}(t) = \hat{k}(0)e^{\lambda t} > 0$ where $f'[e^{-\lambda t}\hat{k}(t)] = \lambda + \gamma$, that is, the marginal product of capital (interest rate), $f'[e^{-\lambda t}k(t)]$, equals the golden-age growth rate, $\lambda + \gamma$. We assume hereafter that a Golden Rule path exists.

In addition to the constraint *(42)*, we have the initial condition

$$k(0) = k_o, \quad k_o > 0. \qquad (43)$$

Equations *(42)* and *(43)* are constraints in the problem of optimal saving.

Under what conditions on preferences, given the above model of production, will it be optimal, when $k_o = \hat{k}(0)$, to follow the Golden Rule of Accumulation or, when $k_o \neq \hat{k}(0)$, to approach the Golden Rule path asymptotically? Ivor Pearce,[32] in response to my Golden Rule essay, asked the related question: if the economy happened initially to be on the Golden Rule path, i.e., $k_o = \hat{k}(0)$, and bound itself to end on the Golden Rule path at some $T > 0$, i.e., $k(T) = \hat{k}(T)$, thus possibly fulfilling some obligation to future generations, would society find it optimal to maintain the economy on the Golden Rule path throughout the intervening time, i.e., equate $k(t)$ to $\hat{k}(t)$ for all t, $0 \leq t \leq T$? Pearce then produced a utility function such that society, to maximize utility in the interval, would have to depart from the Golden Rule path—such that obedience to the Golden Rule would not be optimal, despite the favorable end-point conditions. Specifically he showed that if the social utility function were

$$U(T) = \int_0^T c(t)\, dt, \qquad (44)$$

implying constant marginal utility of per capita consumption, then society would want (until T) to deepen capital in excess of the Golden Rule path, driving the interest rate down to γ (below the Golden Rule level $\lambda + \gamma$) as quickly as possible and remaining on that (different) golden-age path until T at which point the capital in excess of the Golden Rule level, $L(T)\hat{k}(T)$, is instan-

---

[32] Pearce, *op. cit.*

taneously consumed.[33] (Note that as T is increased sufficiently, the economy will spend an arbitrarily large fraction of the time on this path, so that it constitutes the "turnpike," given (44).)

Hence, if the utility function is that in (44), it cannot be optimal to follow the Golden Rule for infinite time since it cannot be optimal to follow that path for any finite interval of time. (In fact I believe it can be shown that, in the untruncated problem where we let $T \rightarrow \infty$, there exists no optimum policy at all, when (44) is the basis for choosing among consumption programs.)

Pearce's analysis suggests the question, under what condition on the utility-rate function will it be optimal to follow the Golden Rule for a finite interval, given that the economy begins and ends on the Golden Rule path? Consider the following class of utility functions:

$$U(T) = \int_0^T e^{-\rho t} u[c(t)] \, dt, \, u'(c) > 0, \, u''(c) < 0. \quad (45)$$

Under what conditions on ρ and u will maximization of (45) subject to (42) and (43) make $k(t) = \hat{k}(t)$, $0 \leq t \leq T$, when $k_o = \hat{k}(0)$, $k(T) = \hat{k}(T)$?

The Euler condition (which is sufficient as well as necessary for a maximum since u is a strictly concave function of the variables $k(t)$ and $\dot{k}(t)$) is

$$\left[\frac{d}{dt} \, u'(c) \right] \bigg/ u'(c) = -(r_t - \gamma - \rho) \quad (46)$$

where

$$r_t = f'[e^{-\lambda t} k(t)].$$

Differentiating $u'(c)$ with respect to time, we find that this equation may be written

$$E(c) \frac{\dot{c}}{c} = -(r_t - \gamma - \rho) \quad (47)$$

---

[33] Why not drive r down to zero? When $r = \gamma$, the sacrifice of a unit of *per capita* consumption initially can permit just a one-unit increase of *per capita* consumption later so that it does not pay to make the sacrifice, thus driving r below γ. (Recall also that the implicit discount rate on *individual* utility rates implied by a function like (44) is equal to γ.)

where

$$E(c) = \frac{u''(c)c}{u'(c)} = \text{elasticity of marginal utility} < 0.$$

Now on the Golden Rule path

$$r_t = \hat{r} = \lambda + \gamma \qquad (48)$$

and

$$\frac{\dot{c}}{c} = \frac{\dot{\hat{c}}}{\hat{c}} = \lambda. \qquad (49)$$

Putting *(47)*, *(48)*, and *(49)* together we obtain

$$E(c) \cdot \lambda = -\lambda + \rho. \qquad (50)$$

Since $\lambda > 0$ here, it follows that $E(c)$ must be a constant, say E. Hence for the optimality of the Golden Rule path in the present end-point problem it is required that $u(c)$ and ρ satisfy

$$\rho = \lambda(1 + E) \quad \text{or} \quad E = -1 + \frac{\rho}{\lambda}. \qquad (51)$$

(Where $\lambda = 0$ one would require $\rho = 0$ and no restrictions on $E(c)$, as we learned in the previous section.)

It has been shown that, should the economy start on the Golden Rule and be constrained to end on it, it would be optimal to follow the Golden Rule throughout the interval $[0, T]$ if and only if *(51)* is satisfied. Let us now consider the standard Ramsey problem of finding an optimum when there is an infinite time horizon and when the economy starts from an arbitrary initial capital stock.

I shall first study this standard problem for the class of $u(c)$ functions such that the elasticity of marginal utility is constant: $E(c) = E = \text{constant} < 0$. Then

$$u'(c) = \alpha c^E, \quad E < 0, \quad \alpha > 0. \qquad (52)$$

The following propositions will be developed:

A.   If $\rho \geq \lambda(1 + E)$ *(or equivalently $E \leq -1 + \rho/\lambda$) an optimum exists. Hence, if we should wish to "treat individuals equally," meaning $\rho = -\gamma$, an optimum exists if $E \leq -1 - \gamma/\lambda$. It appears that no optimum exists if $\rho < \lambda(1 + E)$.*

B. *If $\rho = \lambda(1 + E)$, i.e., (51) is satisfied, the optimal path will approach (or coincide with) the golden-age path on which $r = \lambda + \gamma$, i.e., the Golden Rule path.*

C. *If $\rho > \lambda(1 + E)$, the optimal path will approach (or coincide with) the golden-age path on which $r = \lambda + \gamma + \rho - \lambda(1 + E)$, which is the Golden Utility path.*

First we shall cast our constraint equations *(42)* and *(43)* in terms of consumption and capital per unit *augmented* labor $(e^{\lambda t}L(t))$. Let $\bar{c}(t)$ and $\bar{k}(t)$ denote these respective variables. Then

$$\bar{c}(t) = c(t)e^{-\lambda t}, \quad \bar{k}(t) = k(t)e^{-\lambda t}. \qquad (53)$$

The Golden Rule relations in these variables are

$$f'[\hat{\bar{k}}] = f'[\hat{k}(t)e^{-\lambda t}] = \lambda + \gamma, \qquad (54)$$

$$\hat{\bar{c}} = \hat{c}(t)e^{-\lambda t} = f[\hat{\bar{k}}] - f'[\hat{\bar{k}}]\hat{\bar{k}}. \qquad (55)$$

From *(42)* one easily derives the new constraint relation

$$\bar{c}(t) + \dot{\bar{k}}(t) = g[\bar{k}(t)] \equiv f[\bar{k}(t)] - (\lambda + \gamma)\bar{k}(t), \quad \bar{c}(t) \geq 0, \qquad (56)$$

and from *(43)*

$$\bar{k}(0) = \bar{k}_o = k_o e^{-\lambda t} = k_o. \qquad (57)$$

Concerning our utility function, there are two cases to be considered: $E = -1$ and $-1 \neq E < 0$. Suppose first that $E = -1$. Then, given *(52)*, $u(c)$ is logarithmic:

$$u(c) = \ln c, \qquad (58)$$

and our utility function is

$$U(T) = \int_0^T e^{-\rho t} \ln c(t) \, dt. \qquad (59)$$

Now if $\rho \leq 0$, maximization of the limit of *(59)* as $T \to \infty$ will raise the familiar divergence problem. Let us instead form the integral V, to be maximized, in which the rate of utility corresponding to the Golden Rule path, $e^{-\rho t} \ln (\hat{c}(t))$ is subtracted from the actual rate of utility, $e^{-\rho t} \ln (c(t))$. Noting that $c(t) = \bar{c}(t)e^{\lambda t}$ by *(53)* we have

$$V = \int_0^\infty [e^{-\rho t} \ln c(t) - e^{-\rho t} \ln \hat{c}(t)]\, dt$$

$$= \int_0^\infty \{\ln [\bar{c}(t)e^{\lambda t}] - \ln [\hat{\bar{c}}e^{\lambda t}]\} e^{-\rho t}\, dt$$

$$\hspace{6cm} (\,60\,)$$

$$= \int_0^\infty \{\ln \bar{c}(t) - \ln \hat{\bar{c}} + \lambda t - \lambda t\} e^{-\rho t}\, dt$$

$$= \int_0^\infty [\ln \bar{c}(t) - \ln \hat{\bar{c}}] e^{-\rho t}\, dt\,.$$

First, if $\rho = 0$ (in which case *(51)* is satisfied for $E = -1$) then the problem of maximizing V in *(60)* subject to *(56)* and *(57)* is identical in form to maximizing V in *(27)* subject to *(23)* and *(24)*: $\bar{c}(t)$ replaces $c(t)$ of the previous section, $\ln \bar{c}(t)$ replaces $u(c(t))$ and $\ln \hat{\bar{c}}$ replaces $\hat{u} = u(\hat{c})$. The integral converges and an optimum exists. By analogy to that problem, the optimal path, when $\rho = 0$ and $E = -1$, approaches the Golden Rule path, $\bar{k}(t) = \hat{\bar{k}}$, if $\bar{k}_o \neq \hat{\bar{k}}$, and follows it continuously if $\bar{k}_o = \hat{\bar{k}}$.[34] Since $E = -1$ here, one sees that this result is consistent with proposition B above.

Before turning to the possibilities $\rho > 0$ and $\rho < 0$ let us consider further the merits of the time-independent logarithmic function

$$U(T) = \int_0^T \ln c(t)\, dt \hspace{2.5cm} (\,61\,)$$

which we have just shown causes the Golden Rule path to be approached. Can it be defended as a reasonable social utility function? This function is implied by the social indifference-curve map proposed by James Tobin to be "intertemporally impartial," given a technology like the one under discussion.[35]

---

[34] That the logarithmic function with $\rho = 0$ would give this result was suggested by R. M. Solow in a lecture at Yale University in 1963.

[35] J. Tobin, "Economic Growth as an Objective of Government Policy," *American Economic Review*, Vol. 54, (May 1964), pp. 1–20, especially, Figure 2, p. 8 and pp. 15–16.

Tobin proposed that a representative social indifference curve between *per capita* consumption at $t = 0$, $c(0)$, and *per capita* consumption at any future date t, $c(t)$, should have the property that the marginal rate of substitution (MRS) should equal the ratio of $c(t)$ to $c(0)$. Thus, on the 45° line from the origin, where $c(0) = c(t)$, the MRS equals one or the marginal rate of time preference (MRS minus one) equals zero; where $c(t) = e^{\lambda t}c(0)$, the MRS equals $e^{\lambda t}$, meaning that the sacrifice of a unit of *per capita* consumption at $t = 0$ requires an increase of $c(t)$ equal to $e^{\lambda t}$ to keep social utility constant. Since the "noncomplementarity" and "stationarity" axioms are implicit in Tobin's proposed indifference map, we have an additive Ramsey-like utility integral like *(45)*; since MRS = 1 when $c(t) = c(0)$, we have $\rho = 0$; and since MRS $= u'[c(0)]/u'[c(t)] = c(t)/c(0)$, we have the logarithmic function *(61)*.

Despite the appeal of the logarithmic function, we should remember that $\rho = 0$ is a controversial postulate for it implies that *individual* future utility rates are being discounted at the rate γ, the population growth rate. Let us proceed then to the possibilities $\rho > 0$ and $\rho < 0$.

If $\rho > 0$, then the V integral again converges and there is an optimum. By analogy to standard results obtained for the case $\lambda = 0$, we can infer that the optimal path approaches a golden-age path on which $r = \lambda + \gamma + \rho$. Since $E = -1$, we see that this result is consistent with proposition C: The Golden Utility path, on which $r = \lambda + \gamma + \rho - \lambda(1 + E)$, is approached asymptotically (or followed continuously if the economy should start on it).

These results for $\rho = 0$ and $\rho > 0$ confirm (for the case $E = -1$) the proposition A, namely that an optimum exists if $\rho \geq \lambda(1 + E)$. If $\rho < \lambda(1 + E)$, i.e., $\rho < 0$ in this case, we encounter the divergence of the integral V. This strongly suggests that no optimum exists when $\rho < \lambda(1 + E)$ although I have not demonstrated this.

Consider now the other case, $-1 \neq E < 0$. Integrating *(52)* in this case we obtain

$$u(c) = \frac{\alpha}{1 + E} c^{1+E} + \beta \qquad (62)$$

where

$$\beta = \begin{cases} u(0) \text{ if } 1 + E > 0 & (E > -1), \\ \overline{u} \text{ if } 1 + E < 0 & (E < -1). \end{cases}$$

In other words, if $E > -1$, the utility-rate function is bounded from below by β and is unbounded from above; if $E < -1$, the function is unbounded from below and bounded from above, $\overline{u}$ being the upper bound, approached asymptotically as $c \to \infty$.

Now we perform again the familiar trick of subtracting from the actual rate of utility, $e^{-\rho t}u[c(t)]$, the (discounted) rate of utility corresponding to the Golden Rule path, thus forming the integral V which is to be maximized subject to *(56)* and *(57)*:

$$
\begin{aligned}
V &= \int_0^\infty \{e^{-\rho t}u[c(t)] - e^{-\rho t}u[\hat{c}(t)]\}\, dt \\
&= \int_0^\infty \left\{ \frac{\alpha}{1+E}\, c(t)^{1+E} + \beta - \frac{\alpha}{1+E}\, \hat{c}(t)^{1+E} - \beta \right\} e^{-\rho t}\, dt \\
&\qquad\qquad\qquad\qquad\qquad\qquad\qquad\qquad\qquad\qquad (63) \\
&= \int_0^\infty \left\{ \frac{\alpha}{1+E}\, [\overline{c}(t)e^{\lambda t}]^{1+E} - \frac{\alpha}{1+E}\, [\hat{\overline{c}}e^{\lambda t}]^{1+E} \right\} e^{-\rho t}\, dt \\
&= \int_0^\infty \left\{ \frac{\alpha}{1+E}\, \overline{c}(t)^{1+E} - \frac{\alpha}{1+E}\, \hat{\overline{c}}^{1+E} \right\} e^{-[\rho - \lambda(1+E)]t}\, dt.
\end{aligned}
$$

If $\rho = \lambda(1 + E)$, so that we are doing no "effective" discounting of the utility of consumption per *augmented* labor, and *(51)* is satisfied (the condition for the optimality of the Golden Rule path in the two-point problem) then we have again the standard problem of the previous section. The integral converges and an optimum exists. The Golden Rule path is approached asymptotically if $\overline{k}_o \neq \hat{\overline{k}}$ and is followed continuously if $\overline{k}_o = \hat{\overline{k}}$. This confirms proposition B.

If $\rho > \lambda(1 + E)$ or equivalently $E \leq -1 + \rho/\gamma$, the integral clearly converges and there is again an optimum. By analogy to the standard result for the corresponding problem without technical progress, the optimal path is either coincident with or asymptotic to a golden-age path on which $r = \lambda + \gamma + \rho - \lambda(1 + E)$, where $\rho - \lambda(1 + E)$ (> 0) is the effective rate of discount of utility of consumption per augmented labor. This is the Golden Utility path. It entails a higher interest rate and smaller capital intensity than does the Golden Rule path, when $\rho > \lambda(1 + E)$. When $\rho = \lambda(1 + E)$, the two paths coincide. Proposition C is confirmed.

Finally, as we have just seen, an optimum exists when $\rho \geq \lambda(1 + E)$, i.e., $E \leq -1 + \rho/\lambda$, which confirms proposition A.

Proposition A is quite interesting for it indicates that *an optimum will exist even if there is "equal treatment of individuals," provided that* E *is algebraically sufficiently small.* As was indicated in the previous section, nondiscounting of *individual* utility rates when the population grows at rate γ implies discounting *per capita* utility, $u(c(t))$, at the rate $-\gamma$, i.e., $\rho = -\gamma$. As proposition A indicates, an optimum will exist, even if $\gamma > 0$, provided $E \leq -1 - \gamma/\lambda$, for then $\rho = -\gamma \geq \lambda(1 + E)$. Further, if $E = -1 - \gamma/\lambda$, then $\rho = -\gamma = \lambda(1 + E)$ and the Golden Rule path will be approached asymptotically. If $E < -1 - \gamma/\lambda$, then $\rho = -\gamma > \lambda(1 + E)$, and the Golden Utility path will be approached. In any case, it is *not* true that "equal treatment of individuals" ($\rho = -\gamma$) necessarily precludes the existence of an optimal accumulation policy when $\lambda > 0$. Koopmans's theorem on this subject postulated that $\lambda = 0$. Note that the requirement $E \leq -1 - \gamma/\lambda$ implies that the required $E \to -\infty$ as $\lambda \to 0$ when $\gamma > 0$; this supports Koopmans's theorem.

Attention has been confined thus far to the class of utility-rate functions, $e^{-\rho t}u[c(t)]$, for which the marginal utility elasticity, $E(c)$, is a constant (E). I shall now describe the results of some work by von Weizsäcker[36] and Inagaki[37] and draw from this some rather general conclusions.

Proposition A indicates that when $\rho = 0$, $E \leq -1$ is sufficient for the existence of an optimum. Von Weizsäcker has proved that, when $\rho = 0$ and $E(c)$ is allowed to vary with c, $E(c) \leq -1$ for all c is a sufficient condition for the existence of an optimum, given the present production model. Since proposition A states, more generally, that $E \leq -1 + \rho/\lambda$ is sufficient for the existence of an optimum, it is a reasonable conjecture, by analogy to von Weizsäcker's theorem, that, when $E(c)$ is variable, $E(c) \leq$

[36] Weizsäcker, *op. cit.*

[37] Inagaki, *op. cit.*

$-1 + \rho/\lambda$ for all c is a sufficient condition for the existence of an optimum. But it is to be doubted that this is a necessary condition.

Presumably, what matters for the existence and asymptotic properties of an optimal accumulation program is the limiting behavior of $E(c)$ as $c \to \infty$. Inagaki studied the present model (specializing unnecessarily to the Cobb-Douglas function), employing two utility functions: one of them having the property that the limit $E(\infty) = 0$ and the other the property that $E(\infty) = -\nu, 0 < \nu < 1$, with $dE(c)/dc > 0$ in both cases. He purported to show that $\rho > \lambda(1 + E(\infty))$ is necessary and sufficient for the existence of an optimum; but the analysis in the present paper strongly suggests that $\rho = \lambda(1 + E(\infty))$ would also admit an optimum, given that $E(\infty)$ is approached from below, for it was shown here that $\rho = \lambda(1 + E)$ is sufficient for an optimum when E is constant. (This is a reiteration of our conjecture in the previous paragraph, given that $dE(c)/dc > 0$.) If, however, $dE(c)/dc < 0$ then it would be reasonable to expect that $\rho > \lambda(1 + E(\infty))$ is necessary and sufficient when $E(\infty)$ exists.

Concerning asymptotic properties of the optimal path, Inagaki showed, given either of his utility functions, that the golden-age path on which $r = \lambda + \gamma + \rho - \lambda(1 + E(\infty))$ will be approached asymptotically. This is the Golden Utility path again with this difference: since $E(c)$ is not a constant in Inagaki's model, the economy, once placed on the Golden Utility path would depart from it, returning to it asymptotically. This result by Inagaki, together with the previous analysis, suggests the following, final conjecture: if $E(\infty)$ exists and if an optimum exists, the optimal path will be asymptotic to the Golden Rule path if and only if $\rho = \lambda(1 + E(\infty))$.

CONCLUDING REMARKS

There are two difficulties associated with the Ramsey approach to optimal economic growth on which I shall comment. One is the possible nonexistence of an optimum. The second is the problem of how the social utility function is to be obtained. (Another difficulty—that the utility functions and production models thus far considered are unrealistic—needs no discussion.)

As was shown, an optimum may fail to exist in a variety of models, even in the model with stationary population and technology. The possibility that no optimum will exist is heightened if society wishes to accord "equal treatment to individuals" when the population grows without bound. Suppose there exists no optimum when individual utility rates are not discounted. What then?

Koopmans believes that one might reasonably abandon such a utility function in view of that consequence. ". . . the problem of optimal economic growth is too complicated, or at least too unfamiliar, for one to feel comfortable in making an *entirely* a priori choice of an optimality criterion before one knows the implications of alternative choices. One may wish to choose between principles on the basis of the results of their application."[38] An issue which this view raises is: should social preferences be invariant to the demographic and technological environment? Koopmans apparently believes that the environment should be allowed to influence preferences. But there will surely be many who disagree.

If one insists upon "equal treatment," despite the nonexistence of an optimum, what program of growth should be adopted? With some reservation, I suggest the following. The V-integral formed by subtracting the Golden Rule utility rate from the actual rate of utility will sort consumption programs into three classes when no optimum exists: those paths which cause the integral to diverge to minus infinity, those paths which cause the integral to converge, and those paths which cause the integral to diverge to plus infinity. The latter class of paths is "infinitely better" than the Golden Rule path and paths in the other classes. My suggestion is to choose arbitrarily a path from this class. My reservation is that if some path other than the Golden Rule path had been used as a reference path in forming a V-integral, the class of "infinitely better" paths would be changed.

The other problem that deserves some discussion is the matter of the social utility function. I feel that, in a democratic society, this function must represent the preferences of those in the body politic, hence only those living at the present time. If this is correct, then there is first the problem of obtaining a social utility

[38] Koopmans, *op. cit.*, p. 226.

function from the (living) individuals' utility functions. Samuelson's social indifference curves require centralized information about individual utility functions; it must be assumed that the government has such information. Second, concerning those individual utility functions, the present generation must know the preferences of future people if it gives weight to their welfare or if it cares about their decisions; even its own future consumption will be affected by future governments representing itself and new generations. Hence this problem is quite a complex one in itself. And the information requirements make such analysis of little value to policy makers.

Is there for policy purposes, an alternative to the Ramsey approach? That is, must an optimal consumption program be computed? Recently, I considered an alternative in which the government follows certain rules of taxation, rules which do not require centralized utility information, leaving total saving ultimately in the hands of the consumer in the market.[39] Would growth then be *Pareto optimal* for the present generation? Unfortunately, there are still considerable information requirements and, in the presence of market imperfections, externalities, and overlap of generations, the fiscal principle studied cannot be defended except as a very crude approximation to a Pareto-optimal policy toward growth. It seems that we do not yet have a tolerable solution of the problem of optimal growth policy.

[39] E. S. Phelps, *Fiscal Neutrality Toward Economic Growth* (New York: McGraw-Hill, 1965).

Part **2**

THE GOLDEN RULE
IN OTHER MODELS

Absorptive Capacity
and the Golden Rule
of Accumulation

This paper explores the implications for the Golden Rule of Accumulation, and hence for efficient economic growth, of the existence of a delay between the construction of new capital goods and their use in production.[1] The latter phenomenon has been discussed widely, especially in the context of less-developed countries, under the heading of "absorptive capacity."

There appear to be two distinct uses of the term "absorptive capacity." One concept involves fixed-proportions models. In these models, absorptive capacity is said to be reached when the stock of capital—both in existence and in use—is sufficiently large to employ the entire labor force. If the labor force or the "effective" or "augmented" labor force is growing, continuously positive net investment will be possible without exceeding absorptive capacity. It will be wasteful to invest permanently in excess of this rate, and a waste of foreign aid to finance investment permanently in excess of this rate. This counsel not to exceed absorptive capacity can be viewed as advice not to maintain the capital stock permanently in excess of the Golden Rule value, for in fixed-proportions models of the conventional sort the path on which there is continuously full employment of both capital and labor is the Golden Rule path.

The second type of absorption problem is dynamic in nature. Because it takes time for newly produced capital goods to be

[1] This paper was stimulated by unpublished work of Branko Horvat in which he contended that the growth path which is designated the Golden Rule path in conventional models is inefficient in models containing absorption difficulties. The formulation here is quite different from Horvat's.

installed and possibly for firms to acquire the labor and knowledge to operate them, there may be a gap between the stock of finished capital goods in existence and the stock of capital goods in use or in full use. Absorptive capacity, *in strictu sensu*, is reached when (at full employment) the stock of capital in existence is so much larger than the capital stock in use that an increase in the former will not produce an increase in the latter for some finite interval of time. *Absorption difficulties*, a weaker concept, will be said to prevail when (at full employment) the capital stock in existence exceeds the capital stock in use.

The analysis below focuses on the latter, dynamic type of absorption problem. I shall confine the analysis to the variable-proportions production function. The model is aggregative and excludes capital-embodied (and labor-embodied) technical progress. It is thus a somewhat unrealistic vehicle for study of the problem but I believe that it captures enough of the absorption phenomenon to be of interest. I begin with the simpler of two models.

ABSORPTIVE DIFFICULTIES

The model begins in a conventional way. The labor force, L, grows exponentially at some nonnegative rate γ:

$$L(t) = L_o e^{\gamma t}, \quad \gamma \geq 0. \qquad (1)$$

Output, Q, is a function of *capital in use*, K, and augmented labor. The rate of labor augmentation is a constant, λ.

$$Q(t) = F[K(t), e^{\lambda t}L(t)], \quad \lambda \geq 0, \ \gamma + \lambda > 0. \qquad (2)$$

The production function exhibits constant returns to scale. Marginal products are everywhere positive, diminishing, and continuous. Labor is required for positive output. Hence, if $k(t)$ denotes the ratio of *capital in use* to augmented labor at time t,

$$k(t) = \frac{K(t)}{e^{(\lambda+\gamma)t}L_o}, \qquad (3)$$

then the production function may be written

$$Q(t) = e^{(\lambda+\gamma)t}L_o f\big(k(t)\big),$$
$$f(0) = 0, f'(k) > 0, \ f''(k) < 0, \ f'(\infty) = 0. \qquad (4)$$

Let X denote *capital in existence* so that $\dot{X} = dX/dt$ is the rate of investment. Then if C denotes consumption,

$$C(t) + \dot{X}(t) = Q(t). \qquad (5)$$

Now let $x(t)$ denote the ratio of *capital in existence* to augmented labor at time t:

$$x(t) = \frac{X(t)}{e^{(\lambda+\gamma)t}L_o}. \qquad (6)$$

Differentiating *(6)* we obtain

$$\frac{\dot{X}(t)}{e^{(\lambda+\gamma)t}L_o} = (\lambda + \gamma)x(t) + \dot{x}(t). \qquad (6a)$$

Hence, dividing both sides of *(5)* by $e^{(\lambda+\gamma)t}L_o$ and using *(4)* and *(6)* we have

$$\frac{C(t)}{e^{(\lambda+\gamma)t}L_o} + [(\lambda + \gamma)x(t) + \dot{x}(t)] = f(k(t)). \qquad (7)$$

Suppose now that the investment-output ratio is a constant, s. Then

$$\frac{C(t)}{e^{(\lambda+\gamma)t}L_o} = \frac{Q(t) - \dot{X}(t)}{e^{(\lambda+\gamma)t}L_o} = (1 - s)f(k(t)), \quad 0 < s \leq 1. \qquad (8)$$

From *(7)* and *(8)* we therefore obtain the following differential equation:

$$\dot{x}(t) = sf(k(t)) - (\lambda + \gamma)x(t). \qquad (9)$$

If $x(t) = k(t)$, as in conventional models, then *(9)* reduces to the standard differential equation for analyzing Solow-type growth models. But I shall suppose that there may be absorption difficulties causing $x(t) > k(t)$.

I postulate the following linear absorption mechanism:

$$\dot{K}(t) = \alpha \cdot [X(t) - K(t)] \qquad (10)$$

or equivalently

$$\frac{\dot{K}(t)}{e^{(\lambda+\gamma)t}L_o} = \alpha \cdot [x(t) - k(t)], \quad \alpha > 0, \ x(t) \geq k(t). \qquad (10a)$$

According to *(10)*, the rate at which capital in existence is absorbed into use is proportional to the gap between the two, the absorption coefficient, α, being a positive constant. The second model will introduce a nonlinear mechanism. The greatest doubt surrounding *(10)* is perhaps the assumption that the growth of the labor force or perhaps the growth of the "efficiency" of the labor force does not serve to increase α over time.

Differentiating *(3)* we obtain

$$\frac{\dot{K}(t)}{e^{(\lambda + \gamma)t}L_o} = (\lambda + \gamma)k(t) + \dot{k}(t). \qquad (11)$$

Equations *(10a)* and *(11)* yield

$$\dot{k}(t) = \alpha x(t) - (\alpha + \lambda + \gamma)k(t). \qquad (12)$$

Equation *(12)* together with *(9)* comprise a system of two differential equations in the variables $x(t)$ and $k(t)$. This system is in equilibrium—a golden-age equilibrium—when $\dot{x}(t) = \dot{k}(t) = 0$ for all t. In equilibrium, therefore, we have, letting g denote $\lambda + \gamma$,

$$0 = sf(k) - gx \qquad (13)$$

$$0 = \alpha x - (\alpha + g)k, \qquad (14)$$

or equivalently

$$x = \frac{sf(k)}{g} \qquad (13a)$$

$$x = \left(\frac{\alpha + g}{\alpha}\right)k. \qquad (14a)$$

These two equations are diagrammed in Figure 5. The diagram shows that a unique equilibrium with $k > 0$, $x > 0$ exists if and only if the curve representing *(13a)* is steeper at the origin than the line representing *(14a)*. Hence such an equilibrium exists if and only if

$$sf'(0) > g\left(\frac{\alpha + g}{\alpha}\right). \qquad (15)$$

As $\alpha \to \infty$ we obtain the analogous condition in the conventional growth model without absorption difficulties, viz., $sf'(0) > g$.

Such an equilibrium is globally stable for all $k(0) > 0$, $x(0) \geq k(0)$, as shown by the arrows in Figure 5 whose directions are determined by *(9)* and *(12)*.

FIGURE 5

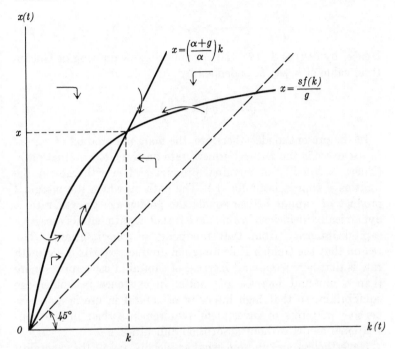

From Figure 5 it can be seen that an increase of the saving ratio leads asymptotically to higher levels of $k(t)$ and $x(t)$, and hence to a higher equilibrium path of output. But after a point, say $\hat{k}$, the Golden Rule level of k, an increase of k due to an increase of s actually reduces consumption, as will now be shown.

From *(7)* we have

$$C(t) = \{f(k(t)) - (\lambda + \gamma)x(t) - \dot{x}(t)\}e^{(\lambda+\gamma)t}L_o. \quad (16)$$

Hence, in golden-age equilibrium, in which $\dot{k}(t) = \dot{x}(t) = 0$, we have

$$C(t) = \{f(k) - (\lambda + \gamma)x\}e^{(\lambda+\gamma)t}L_o. \quad (17)$$

Equating to zero the derivative of $C(t)$ with respect to k, so as to find the consumption-maximizing golden-age path, we find

$$f'(k) - (\lambda + \gamma)\frac{dx}{dk} = 0. \quad (18)$$

From *(13a)* we have

$$\frac{dx}{dk} = \frac{\alpha + g}{\alpha} > 1, \quad g = \lambda + \gamma. \qquad (19)$$

Hence, by *(18)* and *(19)*, the consumption-maximizing or Golden Rule value of k, say $\hat{k}$, is defined by

$$f'(\hat{k}) = g\left(\frac{\alpha + g}{\alpha}\right) > g. \qquad (20)$$

In the present model, therefore, the marginal product of *capital in use* exceeds the natural growth rate on the Golden Rule path. (There is equality of marginal product and growth rate in the limit as α approaches infinity.) The path on which the marginal product of capital in use equals the golden-age growth rate is dynamically inefficient in this model; such a path entails excessive capital intensity from the standpoint of consumption. The reason that the Golden Rule marginal product exceeds the growth rate is that here a one-unit increase of capital in use requires more than a one-unit increase of capital in existence in golden-age equilibrium, so that high intensity of capital in use is more expensive in terms of investment requirements than in the conventional model without absorption difficulties.

Nevertheless one can, somewhat artificially, rescue the generality of the usual formula for the Golden Rule path—equality of capital's marginal product and the golden-age growth rate—by stating that on the Golden Rule path, in either the present or the conventional model, the "marginal product of capital in existence" is equal to the golden-age growth rate. For *(18)* may be written

$$f'(k) \frac{dk}{dx} - (\lambda + \gamma) = 0 \qquad (21)$$

and we can interpret the first term as the equilibrium marginal product of capital in existence.

ABSORPTIVE CAPACITY

In the previous model, absolute absorptive capacity could never be reached: $X(t)$ could never be so large in relation to $K(t)$ that an increase of the former would not immediately increase $\dot{K}(t)$ and hence increase the rate of growth of output. Let us consider a model now in which absorptive capacity could be reached.

In place of *(10)* I postulate the following nonlinear absorption mechanism:

$$\frac{\dot{K}(t)}{e^{(\lambda+\gamma)t}L_o} = \Phi[x(t) - k(t)], \quad \Phi(0) = 0,$$

$$\Phi' > 0, \ \Phi'' < 0 \text{ for } x(t) - k(t) < m \qquad (22)$$

$$\Phi' = 0 \text{ for } x(t) - k(t) \geq m,$$

$$m > 0.$$

This implies that $\dot{K}$ is a linear homogeneous function of X, K, and $e^{gt}L_o$. The rate of absorption per unit effective labor is at a maximum when the gap between $x(t)$ and $k(t)$ equals or exceeds some positive number m. Using *(11)* we may write *(22)* in the form

$$\dot{k}(t) = \Phi[x(t) - k(t)] - (\lambda + \gamma)k(t). \qquad (23)$$

Our two differential equations are now *(9)* and *(23)*. An equilibrium is defined as a path on which $\dot{k}(t) = \dot{x}(t) = 0$ for all t. In equilibrium, therefore,

$$x = \frac{sf(k)}{g} \qquad (24)$$

$$\Phi(x - k) = gk. \qquad (25)$$

Once again a unique equilibrium with $k > 0$ will exist if and only if the curve representing *(24)* is steeper at the origin than the curve representing *(25)*, i.e., if and only if

$$sf'(0) > g\left[\frac{\Phi'(0) + g}{\Phi'(0)}\right]. \qquad (26)$$

This equilibrium can be shown to be globally stable for all $k(0) > 0$.

An increase of the saving ratio once again increases equilibrium x but here it is possible that k will attain an upper bound, given by the vertical portion of the curve depicting *(25)*, so that an increase of s beyond a certain point will not increase equilibrium k, and hence not increase golden-age output. In these equilibria the economy is operating at absorptive capacity. (Of course, $s = 1$ may occur before absorptive capacity is reached.)

Turning to the Golden Rule path, we again use *(17)*, the equation for golden-age consumption, which may be written

$$C(t) = \{f(k) - gx\}e^{gt}L_o. \qquad (27)$$

On the Golden Rule path, as before,

$$f'(k) - g\frac{dx}{dk} = 0. \qquad (28)$$

FIGURE 6

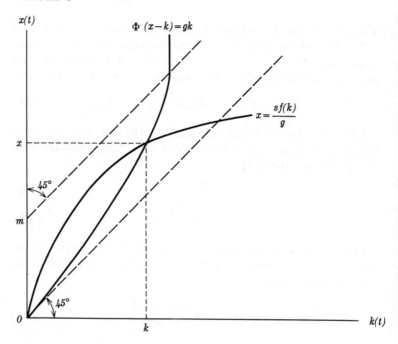

Differentiation of *(25)* yields

$$\frac{dx}{dk} = \frac{\Phi'(x - k) + g}{\Phi'(x - k)} > 1. \qquad (29)$$

Hence, on the Golden Rule path

$$f'(\hat{k}) = g\left[\frac{\Phi'(\hat{x} - \hat{k}) + g}{\Phi'(\hat{x} - \hat{k})}\right] > g. \qquad (30)$$

This condition together with *(25)*, which links x to k, determine the Golden Rule path.

The relation of the Golden Rule path to absorptive capacity may be of some interest. If $\Phi'(x - k)$ is continuous, so that $\Phi'(x - k) \to 0$ as $x - k$ approaches m from below, then the Golden Rule gap, $\hat{x} - \hat{k}$, will be smaller than m; absorptive capacity will not be reached. If $\Phi'(x - k)$ is allowed to be discontinuous, one can conceive of Φ functions which make the Golden Rule $\hat{x}$ the smallest consistent with absorptive capacity.

CONCLUDING REMARKS

The two absorption mechanisms postulated here have the property that an excess of capital in existence over capital in use persists even into long-run, golden-age equilibrium. I briefly consider two absorption mechanisms which do not have this property.

One might postulate that

$$\dot{k}(t) = \Phi[x(t) - k(t)] \qquad (31)$$

or equivalently

$$\frac{\dot{K}(t)}{e^{(\lambda + \gamma)t}L_o} = \Phi[x(t) - k(t)] + (\lambda + \gamma)k(t), \qquad (31a)$$

where Φ has the same properties as in *(22)*.

This mechanism implies that in golden-age equilibrium, where $\dot{k}(t) = 0$, $x(t) = k(t) =$ constant. Hence there is no persistent gap between capital in existence and capital in use. In this model, the Golden Rule path will be characterized by equality between the marginal product of *capital in use* and the golden-age growth rate.

But *(31a)* is not entirely reasonable. Is absorption really faster the greater is the *rate of increase* of the labor force or of the "effective" labor force? It is conceivable that as firms become accustomed to a high γ they learn to absorb new capital faster but I do not find this very plausible. The role of λ in *(31a)* is even more mysterious.

Another absorption mechanism is

$$\frac{\dot{K}(t)}{e^{(\lambda+\gamma)t}L_o} = \Psi[x(t) - k(t), L_o e^{(\lambda+\gamma)t}], \Psi_1, \Psi_2 > 0 \quad (32)$$

with Ψ increasing without bound as the effective labor force increases without bound. This mechanism implies that absorption per unit effective labor is faster the larger the effective labor force, given the gap per unit effective labor. The mechanism suggests that as the effective labor force increases without bound, all capital in existence will tend to be absorbed.

This returns-to-scale mechanism is questionable if population density per land area is constant; for it may be that absorption is actually slower in large countries. Further, *(32)*, like *(22)* and *(31)*, uses *effective* labor; this may be acceptable in production functions but it is less plausible perhaps in absorption equations.

A variety of dynamic absorption mechanisms has been considered. One cannot choose decisively among them without more information about absorption problems than is yet available. This paper has shown that, for some mechanisms, a Golden Rule path may exist and that, expressed in terms of the marginal product of capital in use, the formula for the Golden Rule path differs from that in models without absorption difficulties.

The Golden Rule
of Accumulation
in Rather General
Aggregative "Vintage"
Models

In this essay it will be shown that if there exists an interior consumption-maximizing golden-age path—in short, an interior Golden Rule path—in the general one-commodity vintage model then, on this path, investment equals the earnings of capital and the competitive interest rate equals the rate of growth.

Let us suppose that technical progress is everywhere Harrod neutral; hence it can be described as purely labor augmenting. The rate of labor augmentation is supposed to be constant. Second, we shall suppose that, for simplicity, technical progress is wholly of the capital-embodied type: all technical advances have to be incorporated in new capital goods to raise productivity. Third, we suppose that labor grows geometrically at the rate $\gamma - 1$:

$$L_t = L_o\gamma^t, \quad \gamma > 1. \qquad (1)$$

EX POST AND EX ANTE SUBSTITUTION
POSSIBILITIES IDENTICAL

In the first kind of "vintage" or "embodied" model to be constructed, there is no difference between *ex ante* and *ex post* substitution possibilities, if any, between capital of a given vintage and labor.

In this model, on our previous assumptions, the production function for output produced by labor and capital goods of vintage v is

$$Q_t(v) = F(I_v, \lambda^v L_t(v)), \quad \lambda \geq 1 \qquad (2)$$

where $Q_t(v)$ is output in period t from such capital, I_v is the quantity of capital produced at time v, $L_t(v)$ is the amount of labor working with that capital at time t and $\lambda - 1$ is the rate of (embodied) labor augmentation. We suppose that $F(I_v, \lambda^v L_t(v))$ is nondecreasing and continuous in I_v and $L_t(v)$ and is homogeneous of degree one.

We assume that the investment path is such as to provide enough employment for the total labor force:

$$\sum_{i=1}^{\infty} L_t(t - i) = L_t. \qquad (3)$$

Aggregate output is

$$Q_t = \sum_{i=1}^{\infty} Q_t(t - i). \qquad (4)$$

However we shall be interested in the maximum aggregate output which can be produced. Hence we suppose that

$$Q_t = \max_{\substack{\Sigma L_t(t-i)=L \\ L_t(i) \geq 0}} \left\{ \sum_{i=1}^{\infty} F(I_{t-i}, \lambda^{t-i} L_t(t - i)) \right\}. \qquad (5)$$

That is, labor is allocated to maximize aggregate output.

On these assumptions we can express aggregate output as a function of all the independent variables of the problem:

$$Q_t = P(I_{t-1}, I_{t-2}, \ldots ; L_t; \lambda). \qquad (6)$$

Let us assume now that if, for all i, $I_{t-i} = I_t(1 + g)^{-i}$ where $g = \gamma\lambda - 1$ then $Q_{t-i} = Q_t(1 + g)^{-i}$ for all i. That is, if I_t has always been growing geometrically at the "natural" growth rate then Q_t will also be growing at that same rate. We assume the existence of such golden age paths for all I_t, $0 \leq I_t \leq Q_t$.[1]

[1] See Ken-Ichi Inada, "Economic Growth under Neutral Technical Progress," *Econometrica*, Vol. 32 (January–April 1964), pp. 101–121. Inada (p. 103) has asserted that from *(1)–(5)* we can deduce the stronger proposition

$$Q_t = H(I_{t-1}, I_{t-2}, \ldots ; \lambda^t L_t) \qquad (6a)$$

If investment grows at this "natural" rate then *(6)* and the definition of consumption $C(t) = Q(t) - I(t)$, imply

$$C_t = P(I_t(1 + g)^{-1}, I_t(1 + g)^{-2}, \ldots ; L_t; \lambda) - I_t. \qquad (7)$$

To find that golden-age path which maximizes consumption, assuming an interior maximum to exist, we equate to zero the derivative of C_t with respect to I_t. This yields:

$$\frac{\partial C_t}{\partial I_t} = \sum_{i=1}^{\infty} \frac{\partial P}{\partial I_{t-i}} (1 + g)^{-i} - 1 = 0 \qquad (8)$$

or

$$\sum_{i=1}^{\infty} \frac{\partial P}{\partial I_{t-i}} (1 + g)^{-i} = 1.$$

The expression $\partial P/\partial I_{t-i}$ denotes the marginal productivity of capital of vintage $t - i$ so that $(\partial P/\partial I_{t-i}) I_{t-i}$ is the quasi-rent which is earned by capital of that vintage. Hence capital's relative share is given by

$$a = \sum_{i=1}^{\infty} \frac{\partial P}{\partial I_{t-i}} sQ_{t-i} \bigg/ Q_t = s \sum \frac{\partial P}{\partial I_{t-i}} (1 + g)^{-i} \qquad (9)$$

where we have used $sQ_{t-i} = I_{t-i}$ and $(1 + g)^{-i} = Q_{t-i}/Q_t$.

Equations *(8)* and *(9)* together imply

$$s = a, \qquad (10)$$

that is, if $\partial C_t/\partial I_t = 0$ then golden-age investment equals capital's relative share.

James Tobin has supplied the following proof that the equality in *(10)* is equivalent to equality of the rate of interest and the rate of growth, which is the other way to characterize the Golden Rule path. First, we assume that the one-period rate of interest is equal in a golden age to Keynes's marginal efficiency of capital. The latter is defined as the value of r such that

$$V(r) = 1 \qquad (11)$$

---

which he states is homogeneous of degree one in all variables. If this is correct, as undoubtedly it is, then it follows that if $I_t = I_o(1 + g)^t$ for all t where $g = \gamma\lambda - 1$, then, since $\lambda^t L_t$ is also growing at the rate g, Q_t will also grow at rate g. Hence we may apparently take our assumption as proved.

where

$$V(r) \equiv \sum_{i=1}^{\infty} p_i (1 + r)^{-i},$$

in which p_i denotes the rental rate on a unit of new capital i periods in the future.

Second, we assume that the rental rate on a unit of capital i periods old is constant over time in a golden age. Therefore $p_i = \partial P / \partial I_{t-i}$ for all i and t in a golden age. In other words, the rental rate on capital currently i years old is equal to the rental rate which new capital will be expected to earn when it is i years old. Hence

$$V(r) = \sum_{i=1}^{\infty} \frac{\partial P}{\partial I_{t-i}} (1 + r)^{-i}. \qquad (12)$$

Using this formula for V we obtain, on assigning r the value g,

$$V(g) = \sum_{i=1}^{\infty} \frac{\partial P}{\partial I_{t-i}} (1 + g)^{-i}. \qquad (13)$$

Hence, if the economy is on the interior Golden Rule path, so that $a = s$, then $V(g) = 1$ but this and *(11)* imply that $g = r$. Therefore, in the golden age in which $a = s$, $r = g$. Q.E.D.

Thus we see that, in this vintage model, if there exists a golden-age path in which $a = s$, and hence $r = g$, then this path is the consumption-maximizing golden-age path.

Example: The Vintage Cobb-Douglas Model

Robert Solow[2,3] has shown that if the production function for capital of vintage v is

$$Q_t(v) = B_o e^{\mu t} (e^{tv} I_v)^{\alpha} (L_t(v))^{1-\alpha} \qquad (14)$$

[2] R. M. Solow, "Investment and Technical Progress," in *Mathematical Methods in the Social Sciences*, 1959, edited by K. J. Arrow, Karlin and Suppes, Stanford: Stanford University Press, 1960, pp. 89–104.

[3] It may seem at first that technical progress is not labor augmenting here. But the multiplicative character of the Cobb-Douglas function makes it possible to place the exponential terms as coefficients of the labor term. Thus, in the Cobb-Douglas function there is no possibility of non-Harrod neutral technical progress.

then the following aggregate production function can be derived

$$Q_t = B_o e^{\mu t} J_t^\alpha L_t^{1-\alpha} \qquad (15)$$

where

$$J_t = \int_{-\infty}^t e^{\iota v} I_v \, dv.$$

In a golden age, therefore

$$Q_0 e^{gt} = B_o e^{\mu t} \left[\int_{-\infty}^t e^{\iota v} I_0 e^{gv} \, dv \right]^\alpha [L_o e^{\gamma t}]^{1-\alpha} \qquad (16)$$

which, upon integrating and writing $I_o = sQ_o$, yields

$$Q_0 e^{gt} = B_o e^{\mu t} \left[\frac{sQ_0 e^{(\iota+g)t}}{\iota + g} \right]^\alpha [L_o e^{\gamma t}]^{1-\alpha}. \qquad (17)$$

It follows from *(17)* that

$$g = \frac{\mu}{1 - \alpha} + \frac{\alpha \iota}{1 - \alpha} + \gamma$$

and that

$$Q_0 = \left[\frac{B_o^{1/\alpha} s}{\iota + g} \right]^{\alpha/(1-\alpha)} L_o. \qquad (18)$$

The golden-age consumption level at time zero is therefore

$$C_0 = (1 - s)s^{\,\alpha/1-\alpha} \left[\frac{B_o^{1/\alpha}}{\iota + g} \right]^{\alpha/(1-\alpha)} L_o. \qquad (19)$$

Equating the derivative of C_0 with respect to s equal to zero we find that $s = \alpha$ when C_0 is maximized. Of course, α is capital's relative share if labor is paid its marginal product; for, from the aggregate production function,

$$\frac{\partial Q_t}{\partial L_t} \frac{L_t}{Q_t} = (1 - \alpha).$$

It can also be shown that on the Golden Rule path the rate of return to saving (and the competitive rate of interest) is equal to the golden-age growth rate.

Example: The Vintage Harrod-Domar Model

In this model the vintage production function is

$$Q_t(v) = \min\left[\alpha I_v, \beta e^{\lambda v} L_t(v) \right]. \qquad (20)$$

This model has been studied by Inada[4] and by Solow *et al.*[5] The model is interesting because, despite the lack of substitutability between labor and capital of a given vintage, the model behaves in a neoclassical way: factor shares are always determinate and, if technical progress is purely labor augmenting as *(20)* specifies, there exist golden-age paths for a wide range of saving-income ratios.

Solow *et al.* have proved that if there exists a golden age in which the saving ratio equals capital's relative share or, equivalently, the competitive rate of interest equals the golden-age growth rate, then that path is the Golden Rule path: it maximizes consumption. The reader is referred to their paper for the proof.

NO *EX POST* SUBSTITUTION

We have thus far considered only the kind of vintage model in which there is no difference between *ex ante* and *ex post* substitutability. One-commodity models in which there *is* a difference have been constructed by Leif Johansen[6] and by the present author.[7] Perhaps the hallmark of this kind of vintage model is that the amount of output currently producible from capital of vintage v depends upon the labor intensity of the production process initially chosen so that it is a function of the labor initially used to produce that output, $L_v(v)$:

$$Q_v(v) = F(I_c, e^{\lambda v}L_v(v)),$$
$$Q_t(v) = G(I_v, e^{\lambda v}L_t(v); L_v(v)). \qquad (21)$$

An implication of this feature of the model is that current aggregate output will depend upon the entire past history of the

[4] Inada, *op. cit.*

[5] R. M. Solow, J. Tobin, C. C. von Weizsäcker, and M. Yaari, "Neoclassical Growth with Fixed Factor Proportions, "*Review of Economic Studies*, Vol. 33 (April 1966), pp. 79–116.

[6] L. Johansen, "Substitution versus Fixed Production Coefficients in the Theory of Economic Growth: A Synthesis," *Econometrica*, Vol. 28 (April 1959), pp. 157–176.

[7] E. S. Phelps, "Substitution, Fixed Proportions, Growth and Distribution," *International Economic Review*, Vol. 4 (September 1963), pp. 265–288.

independent variables of the economy. It is no longer possible to represent current output as a function of current labor, the history of the technology, and the history of investment; we must consider also the history of the labor force. If labor has always been growing geometrically, however, we can do this simply by introducing labor's growth rate into our "production function":

$$Q_t = P(I_{t-1}, I_{t-2}, \ldots ; L_o, \gamma, \lambda). \qquad (22)$$

We can then apply the same argument as earlier to prove that if there is a golden-age path with equality of the saving ratio and capital's relative share, then this path is the consumption-maximizing golden-age path or Golden Rule path.

Example: The Cobb-Douglas-Johansen Model

Johansen[8] developed a model in which no *ex post* substitution takes place: either $L_t(v) = L_v(v)$ so that $Q_t(v) = Q_v(v)$ or else $L_t(v) = 0$ so that $Q_t(v) = 0$. The present author[9] developed the model further by providing a theory of when capital of a given vintage would be utilized and proceeded to show how the retirement age of capital goods depended upon the various parameters of the model. It was shown that a golden age existed for every constant saving-income ratio and that in the consumption-maximizing golden age the rate of interest equals the golden-age growth rate and the saving ratio equals capital's relative share. The reader is referred to that paper for the proof.

CONCLUDING REMARKS

The models discussed here are not entirely general aggregative models. Technical progress may be labor-embodied as well as capital-embodied and disembodied. Second, *ex post* substitutability may exist but be less than *ex ante* substitutability, as in the textbook case.[10] Neither extension of the vintage model will affect the characterization of the Golden Rule path.

---

[8] Johansen, *op. cit.*

[9] Phelps, *op. cit.*

[10] See S. Y. Park, "Bounded Substitution, Fixed Proportions and Economic Growth," Doctoral Dissertation, Yale University, 1965.

Induced Invention
and the Golden Rule

One of the most remarkable empirical regularities in a great many economies for which we have adequate data is the near constancy of the ratio of wages (and of profits) to national income. Contemporary growth theory has illuminated the phenomenon to some degree with the construction of models in which there exists a stable, equilibrium golden-age growth path.[1] In a golden age, factor shares are constant, their magnitudes usually depending upon the saving-income ratio, the population growth rate, and the technological parameters.

But this kind of growth model does not really solve the puzzle of factor share constancy. For a golden-age path can exist, in aggregative models, only if technical progress going on happens to be Harrod neutral. Further, in showing the stability of the equilibrium golden-age path, it is usually postulated that progress is Harrod neutral for *all* capital-labor ratios so that progress can be described as purely labor augmenting.[2] Thus one is led to ask why progress should be assumed to be Harrod neutral, either in or out of equilibrium.

[1] See especially R. M. Solow, "A Contribution to the Theory of Economic Growth," *Quarterly Journal of Economics*, Vol. 70 (February 1956), pp. 65–94; and H. Uzawa, "Neutral Inventions and the Stability of Growth Equilibrium," *Review of Economic Studies*, Vol. 28 (February 1961), pp. 117–124.

[2] A little-known generalization of this model may be mentioned. If there is positive capital augmentation at a constant rate and the saving ratio declines exponentially at that same rate then, on standard assumptions, there will exist a stable "growth equilibrium" with constant factor shares and exponential output growth and superexponentially growing consumption. Such a model fits the facts of United States growth better than the pure labor-augmentation model.

Evidently, a satisfactory model of the evolution of factor shares and of productivity requires a satisfactory theory of the factor-saving character of technical progress. A complete theory came in sight with the recent publication of a contribution by Charles Kennedy.[3] Introduced there is what will be called here the *invention possibility frontier*. This postulated frontier fully characterizes the alternative new isoquants that firms know to be producible through invention, given the current isoquant. Combined with this concept is a maximization postulate that may be a good first approximation, namely that firms seek to maximize, subject to the frontier, the current rate of cost reduction—hence the current rate or intensity of technical progress—taking no interest in the factor-saving bias of technical progress *per se*.

From these and other postulates, Kennedy argues the existence of various golden-age equilibrium paths, one for each saving ratio, all of which yield the same distribution of income between wages and profits. In these equilibria, factor shares depend only upon the shape of the invention possibility frontier (at a particular point), not upon relative factor supplies (hence the saving ratio) nor upon the elasticity of substitution as conventional growth theory holds.

However, Kennedy failed to articulate sufficiently the underlying production side of the model—apparently a fixed-proportions production function—nor on what principle (e.g., marginal productivities) income is distributed to capital and labor. Further, he omitted any demonstration of the stability of golden-age equilibrium, or of the conditions for stability.

A joint paper by Emmanuel Drandakis and the present author, stimulated by the work of Kennedy, offers a complete (aggregative) model of growth and distribution utilizing the notion of induced invention.[4] A brief description of this model and the

---

[3] C. Kennedy, "Induced Innovation and the Theory of Distributive Shares," *Economic Journal*, Vol. 74 (September 1964), pp. 541–547. Unpublished work by C. C. von Weizsäcker was remarkably similar in its basic concepts.

[4] E. M. Drandakis and E. S. Phelps, "A Model of Induced Invention, Growth and Distribution," forthcoming *Economic Journal*. A somewhat similar and independent paper by P. A. Samuelson is more general in some respects and more restrictive in others. See P. A. Samuelson, "A Theory of Induced Innovation along Kennedy-Weizsäcker Lines," *Review of Economics and Statistics*, Vol. 47 (November 1965), pp. 343–356.

principal results from it now follow. Then the Golden Rule path is shown to exist in this model.

The production function is neoclassical with constant returns to scale. Technical progress is factor augmenting. Hence,

$$Q(t) = F[B(t)K(t), A(t)L(t)]. \qquad (1)$$

Over time, firms employ exogeneously supplied inventors to increase A or B over time. The rates of factor augmentation, $\dot{A}/A$ and $\dot{B}/B$, are thus endogenous variables of the model. Firms are supposed to direct inventive effort, i.e., choose rates of factor augmentation, so as to maximize at each moment of time the rate of competitive cost reduction, or equivalently, the "rate" of technical progress, R:

$$R = a\frac{\dot{B}}{B} + (1-a)\frac{\dot{A}}{A} \qquad (2)$$

where

$$a = \frac{BF_1K}{F} = \text{capital's competitive share.}$$

This maximization is performed subject to the constraint of the invention possibility frontier, which takes the form

$$\frac{\dot{A}}{A} = \varphi\left(\frac{\dot{B}}{B}\right), \ \varphi(0) > 0, \ \varphi' < 0, \ \varphi'' < 0, \qquad (3)$$

as pictured in Figure 7. This strictly convex frontier is constant over time and invariant to the capital-labor ratio, hence invariant to factor prices and shares.[5]

To maximize R in *(2)* subject to *(3)*, we substitute *(3)* into *(2)*, and differentiate R totally with respect to $\dot{B}/B$ and equate this

[5] A widely circulated draft of the Drandakis–Phelps paper (Cowles Foundation Discussion Paper 186, July 1965) posits that the frontier lies everywhere in the positive quadrant, i.e., $\dot{A}, \dot{B} \geq 0$. For if we want the chosen invention to imply nonnegative technical progress (R) for *all* capital-labor ratios and all production functions, we cannot allow any negative factor augmentation. But this restriction comes at a high price and is especially undesirable in the present context where it is convenient to allow negative capital augmentation.

FIGURE 7

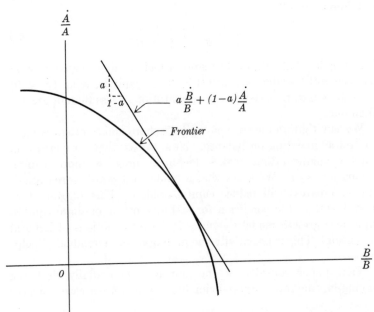

derivative to zero, which yields a necessary and sufficient condition for the "optimal" rate of capital augmentation:

$$\varphi'\left(\frac{\dot{B}}{B}\right) = \frac{-a}{1-a}. \qquad (4)$$

This solution is illustrated in Figure 7.

By geometrical analysis using Figure 7 or by differentiation of (4) one finds that an increase of a increases optimal $\dot{B}/B$ and decreases optimal $\dot{A}/A$:

$$\frac{d(\dot{B}/B)}{da} > 0, \ \frac{d(\dot{A}/A)}{da} < 0. \qquad (5)$$

Thus technical progress will be algebraically more capital augmenting on balance the larger is capital's share.

Defining, as is customary, the Hicksian bias of technical progress, $\widetilde{B}$, as the proportionate time rate of increase of the marginal product of capital less the proportionate growth rate of the marginal product of labor at a given capital-labor ratio, we obtain the well-known result

$$\widetilde{B} = \frac{1 - \sigma}{\sigma} \left(\frac{\dot{A}}{A} - \frac{\dot{B}}{B} \right). \qquad (6)$$

This implies that technical progress which is labor augmenting on balance will be labor saving ($\widetilde{B} > 0$) or capital saving ($\widetilde{B} < 0$) according as σ, the elasticity of substitution, is less than or greater than one.

We saw that an increase of capital's share makes progress more capital augmenting on balance. Now we see that an increase in capital augmentation makes technical progress more capital saving if $\sigma < 1$. We know that a tendency toward more capital-saving progress will reduce capital's share. This suggests that $\sigma < 1$ will be the condition for stability of factor-share equilibrium in a growth model that uses the present notions of induced invention. This is essentially the finding of the Drandakis-Phelps paper.

That paper considers a constant or exponentially declining saving-income ratio. Specializing here to the former case, we have

$$\dot{K}(t) = sQ(t), \quad 0 < s \leq 1. \qquad (7)$$

In addition, exponential labor growth is postulated:

$$\dot{L}(t) = \gamma L(t), \quad \gamma > 0, \ L_o > 0. \qquad (8)$$

From this system of equations one then obtains the needed pair of differential equations

$$\dot{a} = a(1 - a) \left[\widetilde{B}(a) - \frac{1 - \sigma}{\sigma} (\hat{K} - \gamma) \right] \qquad (9)$$

$$\dot{\hat{K}} = \hat{K}[R(a) - (1 - a)(\hat{K} - \gamma)] \qquad (10)$$

where $\hat{K} \equiv \dot{K}/K$ and where $\widetilde{B}(a)$ and $R(a)$ are functions of a according to the induced-invention theory just outlined. Equilibrium occurs when $\dot{a} = \dot{\hat{K}} = 0$, i.e., a and $\hat{K}$ are constants, a^* and $\hat{K}^*$ respectively where $\hat{K}^* > 0, 0 < a^* < 1$. (In equilibrium, σ is necessarily constant over time.) From *(9)* and *(10)* one obtains, upon making the appropriate substitutions for $\widetilde{B}$ and R

from *(2)* and *(6)*, the following equations in the equilibrium values:

$$\frac{\dot{B}}{B} (a^*) = 0 \qquad (11)$$

$$\hat{K}^* = \varphi(0) + \gamma. \qquad (12)$$

That is, the equilibrium value of capital's share is such as to make the optimal rate of capital augmentation equal to zero. The corresponding optimal rate of labor augmentation, $\varphi(0)$, plus γ, give the equilibrium rate of growth of capital and of output. Hence the standard golden-age equilibrium with pure labor augmentation and constant shares is obtained. This equilibrium is shown, with minor qualification, to be globally stable for all initial states if and only if $\sigma < 1$ for all capital-labor ratios. Thus Kennedy's propositions are supported (if $\sigma < 1$), in a neoclassical model that posits marginal-productivity factor pricing.

THE GOLDEN RULE

There is no analysis by Drandakis and Phelps of the equilibrium paths of output, capital, and consumption, only the equilibrium growth rates. To show the existence and characteristics of the Golden Rule path, one needs to know how the "level" of the exponentially growing consumption path depends upon capital intensity.

First, it is necessary to recognize that the equilibrium paths of $B(t)$ and of $A(t)$ depend upon $K(t)$. Writing the production function *(1)* in the form

$$\frac{Q(t)}{A(t)L(t)} = f(k(t)) \qquad (1a)$$

where

$$k(t) = \frac{B(t)K(t)}{A(t)L(t)}$$

and

$$f(k(t)) = F[k(t), 1]$$

we have

$$\frac{BF_1K}{F} = \frac{f'(k)k}{f(k)} = a^* = \text{constant} \qquad (13)$$

in every golden age. Hence k takes the same value, say k^*, in every golden-age equilibrium. Letting λ denote $\varphi(0)$, the rate of labor augmentation in golden-age equilibrium, we have in any golden age

$$\frac{B(t)}{A(t)} = \frac{B_0}{A_0 e^{\lambda t}} = k^* \frac{L(t)}{K(t)} = k^* \frac{L_o e^{\gamma t}}{K_0 e^{(\gamma+\lambda)t}} = k^* \frac{L_o}{K_0 e^{\lambda t}}. \quad (14)$$

Hence the ratio B_0/A_0 in golden-age equilibrium is functionally related to the K_0 that prevails (at reference time zero) in the golden age. B_0/A_0 is a function only of K_0, given k^* which is a constant in this context.

Now it can be argued that B_0 and A_0 are each functions only of K_0, for K_0 is really the only state variable needed to characterize the prevailing golden age at time zero. Hence we may write

$$B_0 = B(K_0), \ A_0 = A(K_0). \quad (15)$$

The preceding model indicates that $B'(K_0) < 0$ and $A'(K_0) > 0$ on the stability assumption that $\sigma < 1$. For suppose that the economy is initially on some golden-age path, whereupon the saving ratio is increased. This increases the growth rate of capital and hence, if $\sigma < 1$, depresses capital's share. The fall of capital's share increases $\dot{A}/A$ while reducing $\dot{B}/B$ (hence making $\dot{B}/B$ negative). Gradually, however, the capital-growth rate falls back to the "natural," golden-age growth rate, with the "level" of the capital stock now higher, while $\dot{A}/A$ returns to the value λ and $\dot{B}/B$ returns to the value zero, $A(t)$ now at a higher "level" and $B(t)$ at a lower (constant) level. Hence, the move to a golden age with more saving and more capital is associated with an upward shift of the $A(t)$ path and a downward shift of the $B(t)$ path. Hence, large K_0 is associated with large A_0 and small B_0.

Which golden age, i.e., which K_0, is associated with the highest consumption path, if a consumption maximum should exist? In a golden age, consumption at time t, $C(t)$, is given by

$$\begin{aligned} C(t) = \{F[B(K_0)K_0 e^{(\gamma+\lambda)t}, A(K_0)e^{\lambda t}L_o e^{\gamma t}] \\ - (\gamma + \lambda)K_0 e^{(\gamma+\lambda)t}\} \end{aligned} \quad (16)$$

where

$$(\gamma + \lambda)K_0 e^{(\gamma+\lambda)t} = \dot{K}(t).$$

Differentiating with respect to K_0 and equating the derivative to zero yields

$$\{B_0 F_1 - (\gamma + \lambda) + [B'(K_0)F_1 K_0 \\ + A'(K_0)F_2 L_o]\} e^{(\gamma+\lambda)t} = 0. \quad (17)$$

It is clear from this equation that there may exist a value of K_0 which causes the left-hand side of (17) to be equal to zero for all t. Thus there may very well be a Golden Rule path in this induced-invention model. More about existence conditions will be said later.

How may the Golden Rule path, should it exist, be characterized? If the bracketed expression (within the brace) in (17) is zero, we have

$$B_0 F_1 = \gamma + \lambda. \quad (18)$$

This is the standard characterization of the Golden Rule path, that it equates the marginal product of capital to the golden-age rate of growth. I shall argue now that the aforementioned bracketed expression is indeed equal to zero.

It can be seen that

$$B'(K_0)F_1 K_0 + A'(K_0)F_2 L_o$$

$$= \left\{ \frac{F_1 B_0 K_0}{Q_0} \frac{B'(K_0)K_0}{B_0} + \frac{F_2 A_0 L_o}{Q_0} \frac{A'(K_0)K_0}{A_0} \right\} \frac{Q_0}{K_0} \quad (19)$$

$$= \left\{ a^* \frac{dB_0}{dK_0} \frac{K_0}{B_0} + (1 - a^*) \frac{dA_0}{dK_0} \frac{K_0}{A_0} \right\} \frac{Q_0}{K_0}.$$

We would like to show that the right-hand side of (19) is equal to zero.

The induced-invention model causes the rates of factor augmentation to maximize continuously the rate of technical progress and hence, for any given paths of $K(t)$ and $L(t)$, to maximize the rate of growth of $Q(t)$. It must be, therefore, that in the equilibrium golden-age state the "level" of output is maximized; for if it were not it would be possible to choose a different, nonequilibrium point on the invention possibility frontier which would yield (at least temporarily) a growth rate higher than the golden-age growth rate $\gamma + \varphi(0)$.

Now if the paths of $B(t)$ and $A(t)$ are such as to maximize the "level" of the equilibrium output path, hence the values B_0

and A_0 in the equilibrium golden age are such as to maximize $F(B_0K_0, A_0L_o)$, then there is no feasible deviation from these values, dA_0 and dB_0 which will yield a higher F. Hence

$$dQ_0 = F_1K_0\, dB_0 + F_2L_o\, dA_0 = 0 \qquad (20)$$

whence

$$\frac{F_1B_0K_0}{Q_0}\frac{dB_0}{B_0} + \frac{F_2A_0L_o}{Q_0}\frac{dA_0}{A_0} = 0. \qquad (21)$$

This implies that the braced expressions in *(19)* are zero. (This whole argument is of course the familiar one that in maximizing consumption with respect to K_0, A_0, and B_0, we need not worry about the effect that a variation of K_0 has upon optimal A_0 and B_0 since the latter two variables can be varied without effect in the neighborhood of the maximum.)

Since the bracketed expression is zero, equation *(18)* characterizes the Golden Rule path. Hence, in this induced-invention model, no less than in standard models with exogenous labor augmentation, the marginal product of capital is equal to the golden-age growth rate on the Golden Rule path.

Multiplying both marginal product and growth rate in *(18)* by the capital-output ratio, we obtain the other characterization,

$$\frac{B_0F_1K_0}{Q_0} = \frac{(\gamma + \lambda)K_0}{Q_0}, \qquad (22)$$

and therefore

$$s = a^* \qquad (23)$$

where s is the investment-output or saving ratio, and a^*, we recall, is a constant. The invention possibility frontier, as postulated in *(3)*, cuts the vertical (labor-augmentation) axis with finite negative slope, insuring that $0 < a^* < 1$. Hence there necessarily exists a value of the saving ratio, $0 < s < 1$, such that *(23)* is satisfied. Thus, in this induced-invention model, as in the special Cobb-Douglas case of standard model, there necessarily exists a Golden Rule path.

CONCLUDING REMARKS

It seems likely that this model and the Golden Rule concept that emerges from it can be used to study the dynamical efficiency and the social optimality of various growth paths. But it is probable that such difficult extensions of the simple analyses of those matters set forth earlier in this volume are best deferred to such a time as we have a fuller understanding of the connections among the rate and bias of technical progress, distributive shares, inventive effort, and education.

Part **3**

EXTENSIONS OF
THE GOLDEN RULE

Models of Technical
Progress and the
Golden Rule of Research

The primary purpose of this paper is to present a model of technical progress and economic growth from which one can derive a Golden Rule of Research quite analogous to the Golden Rule of Accumulation. The secondary purpose is to discuss various models of technical progress.

That there might exist a Golden Rule for research is not surprising since research is a kind of investment—investment in technology—just as "accumulation" denotes investment in tangible capital. Nevertheless "capital" and "technology" differ in important respects. If, given the technology, the production of commodities is homogeneous of degree one in labor and capital goods, as is frequently postulated, then production cannot be homogeneous of degree one in labor, capital, and "technology" (or the appropriate index of past research effort). Further, the production of technical progress, unlike the production of investment goods, seems unlikely to exhibit constant returns to scale in capital and labor, given the technology. Hence technology cannot be treated as an ordinary capital good. Because of this novelty that our subject presents, this paper must be highly tentative and conjectural.

MODELS OF TECHNICAL PROGRESS

In order to speak about the "level of technology" in an operational way without specifying all details of the production function and in order to make possible the generation of golden ages I postulate that technical progress is purely labor augmenting, hence Harrod neutral. Therefore

$$Q(t) = F(K(t), T(t)N(t)), \qquad (1)$$

where $Q(t)$ denotes the rate of output of the single consumer-capital good of the economy, $K(t)$ the stock of capital, $N(t)$ the rate of employment of ordinary production workers (as distinct from researchers), and $T(t)$ the level of technology, all at time t. Technical progress here is of the "disembodied" kind: old capital and new capital are identical, as are old workers and young workers. It would not affect our results if we were to make our labor-augmenting technical progress "capital-embodied"; and while, to our knowledge, "labor-embodied" technical progress has never been modeled, it seems likely that such embodiment could also be introduced without critical effect.

Second, I suppose that the labor force is homogeneous. No one has an absolute advantage in either research or the production of commodities. Later this assumption will be relaxed.

Finally, I suppose initially that only labor is productive in the research industry; capital, therefore, is not employed to produce technical progress. Thus the level of technology at any particular point of time depends in some way upon past research by the labor force. Let us address ourselves now to the nature of that functional relationship.

There are certain properties which I wish the "technology function" to possess. The first of these properties is *diminishing returns*. Given past research effort, the marginal effectiveness of research decreases with the amount of research done at a particular time. Consider the following technology function, inspired by the frequent assumption that $T(t) = T(0)e^{\lambda t}$:

$$T(t) = T(0)e^{\beta \sum_{v=0}^{t} R(v)}, \quad \beta > 0, \qquad (a)$$

where $R(v)$ denotes the amount of employment in the research industry at time v. This function implies increasing marginal effectiveness of research at time v since $(\partial T(t)/\partial R(v)) = \beta T(t)$ and $T(t)$ is an increasing function of $R(v)$. So we rule out this function.

Second, I require that there should be a loss from bunching a given amount of total research effort in a short interval of time.

This is the condition for *diminishing marginal rate of substitution.* Consider the function proposed by Edwin Mansfield:[1]

$$T(t) = \beta \left[\int_{-\infty}^{t} R(v) \, dv \right]^{\alpha}, \quad 0 < \alpha < 1, \beta > 0. \quad (b)$$

This function exhibits diminishing returns but it implies that the marginal rate of substitution between research at one time and at another for producing the technology level at time t is constant (and unitary) so that there is no premium on a smooth research trend.

The third property I require is that the marginal effectiveness of current research be an increasing function of the level of technology recently attained. We may call this property *technical progress in research.* This is perhaps controversial but it seems plausible that today's researchers have a higher marginal effectiveness than those of a century ago. This does not imply, of course, that the relative rate of technical progress must increase over time with a stationary research trend or even with an exponentially rising research trend. Consider, then, the following technology function which, if $G(R)$ is increasing and strictly concave, implies both diminishing marginal returns and diminishing marginal rate of substitution:

$$T(t) = \int_{-\infty}^{t} G(R(v)) \, dv. \quad (c)$$

This function implies that the marginal-effectiveness function, $G'(R)$, is stationary so that researchers do not get more productive over time. It would be easy to introduce exogenous technical progress in the research industry (and perhaps natural to do so in an open economy) but we prefer to suppose that such technical progress is endogenously produced by the researchers themselves.

The fourth property I require is that *exponential growth of researchers will produce an exponential increase of the level of technology,* provided research has always been growing exponentially at the same rate. Clearly this assumption is motivated by a desire to generate golden ages. I have no evidence with which to attack or defend this assumption; suffice it to say that it is not

---

[1] E. Mansfield, "Rates of Return from Industrial Research and Development," *American Economic Review,* Vol. 55 (May 1965), pp. 310–322.

so farfetched as to merit no analysis. The heuristic value of analyzing golden ages is plain. Consider, then, the following technology function, which meets the first three of our requirements if $H(R, T)$ is increasing in both arguments and strictly concave in R:

$$T(t) = \int_{-\infty}^{t} H(R(v), T(v - \omega))\, dv, \quad \omega > 0. \qquad (d)$$

Here the effectiveness of researchers at time t in producing technical progress at time t is an increasing function of the level of technology at time $t - \omega$. The "retardation," ω, might be interpreted as the "publication lag." But whether this function satisfies my fourth requirement depends upon the nature of $H(R, T)$.

Suppose that the productivity of researchers in producing technical progress at time t is proportional to the level of technology at $t - \omega$. That is, suppose that H is homogeneous of degree one in $T(v - \omega)$:

$$H(R(v), T(v - \omega)) = T(v - \omega)G(R(v)). \qquad (d')$$

Then, since $\dot{T}(t) = H(R(t), T(t - \omega))$,

$$\dot{T}(t) = T(t - \omega)G(R(t))$$

or

$$\frac{\dot{T}(t)}{T(t)} = \frac{T(t - \omega)}{T(t)}\, G(R(t)).$$

This implies that a constant rate of research permits a constant relative rate of increase of the technology level. For, as may be easily verified from the previous equation, if $R(v) = c$ for all v then $\dot{T}(t)/T(t) = r$ in the transcendental equation

$$r = e^{-r\omega}G(c).$$

Further, it is only if $R(v) = c$ that technology will grow exponentially; if $R(v)$ should grow exponentially, $T(t)$ will rise faster than exponentially. Thus (d') fails to satisfy our fourth requirement that exponential growth of research will produce a constant relative rate of technological progress.

Fortunately there is at least one function which will satisfy my four requirements. This is the technology function in *(d)* where it is assumed now that $H(R, T)$ is homogeneous of degree one in both $R(v)$ and $T(v - \omega)$ and that $H(0, T) = 0$. This means that if the technology level should double we would require exactly twice the amount of research to double the absolute time rate of increase of the technology, $\dot{T}(t) = H(R(t), T(t - \omega))$; and that positive technical progress requires positive research. Thus I shall suppose, in supplement to *(d)*, the following:

$$H(R(v), T(v - \omega)) = T(v - \omega)H\left(\frac{R(v)}{T(v - \omega)}, 1\right). \qquad (e)$$

Letting $h(x) = H(x, 1)$ and using $\dot{T}(t) = H(R(t), T(t - \omega))$, we obtain

$$\frac{\dot{T}(t)}{T(t)} = \frac{T(t - \omega)}{T(t)} h\left(\frac{R(t)}{T(t - \omega)}\right). \qquad (e')$$

It can be shown that constant research effort will cause the relative rate of technical progress to approach zero.[2] Constancy of the relative rate of growth of technology, that is, exponential technical progress, occurs if research is exponentially rising and has always done so. Suppose that $R(t) = R(0)e^{\gamma t}$. Then $T(t) = T(0)e^{\gamma t}$ satisfies *(e')*. That is, $\dot{T}/T = \gamma$ is the solution to *(e')*. If we make these substitutions in *(e')* we obtain the transcendental

---

[2] *Proof:* Let $R(v) = c$ for all v. If T were to approach an upper limit then obviously $\dot{T}/T$ would approach zero. Actually, T increases without limit. Hence

$$\lim_{t \to \infty} \frac{\dot{T}(t)}{T(t - \omega)} = \lim_{t \to \infty} h\left(\frac{c}{T(t - \omega)}\right) = 0$$

so that

$$\lim_{t \to \infty} \frac{\dot{T}(t)}{T(t)} \frac{T(t)}{T(t - \omega)} = \lim_{t \to \infty} \frac{\dot{T}(t)}{T(t)} \cdot \lim_{t \to \infty} \frac{T(t)}{T(t - \omega)} = 0.$$

But

$$\lim_{t \to \infty} \frac{T(t)}{T(t - \omega)} > 0.$$

Hence

$$\lim_{t \to \infty} \frac{\dot{T}(t)}{T(t)} = 0.$$

equation

$$\gamma = e^{-\gamma\omega} h\left(\frac{R(0)}{T(0)} e^{\gamma\omega}\right) \qquad (e'')$$

which yields the steady-growth "level" of technology at the reference time point, time zero, as a function of the level of research at that time. Equation *(e'')* implies that a doubling of the "level" of research, without any change of the relative rate of increase of research, is associated with a doubling of the "level" of technology (without changing the relative rate of growth of the technology). This in no way contradicts the diminishing returns requirement for that refers to a *ceteris paribus* variation of research at a single moment of time. Such proportionality is analogous to the proportionality, in golden ages, of the "level" of exponentially growing output to the "level" of the exponentially growing labor force, despite diminishing marginal productivity of labor in the usual sense.

GOLDEN AGES AND GOLDEN RULES

To complete the model we introduce first a full-employment condition

$$R(t) + N(t) = L(t) \qquad (2)$$

where $L(t)$ is the total labor force and $N(t)$ is employment in the production of commodities.

Second, all unconsumed output is invested and there is no depreciation. Hence

$$C(t) + \dot{K}(t) = Q(t) \qquad (3)$$

where $C(t)$ denotes consumption and $\dot{K}(t)$ the rate of increase of capital (hence, the rate of investment).

By definition, in a golden age, the total labor force, researchers, and commodity-producing workers all grow at constant relative rates. This condition together with *(2)* imply that they must grow at the same relative rate. Hence

$$L(t) = L_o e^{\gamma t}, \qquad (4)$$

$$R(t) = R(0)e^{\gamma t}, \quad \gamma > 0, \text{ for all } t \gtreqless 0. \qquad (5)$$

Equations *(2)*, *(4)*, and *(5)* imply that $N(t) = N(0)e^{\gamma t}$ so that the latter is not an independent equation. Note that while $L(0)$ is a historical datum given by the parameter L_o, $R(0)$ is not; the "level" of research effort (even in the infinite past) we imagine to be open to choice.

Equations *(5)*, *(d)* and *(e)* imply, as we showed in the previous section, that technology grows exponentially at rate γ and that the "level" of technology at time zero is proportional to the level of research at that time. Hence we may write

$$T(t) = \eta R(0)e^{\gamma t}, \quad \eta > 0. \qquad (6)$$

Note that if there exist technology functions other than *(d)* and *(e)* which, with *(5)*, imply *(6)*, then the following analysis will apply to them as well as the technology function we have adopted.

Equations *(1)* through *(6)* contain seven unknown variables: $L(t)$, $R(t)$, $N(t)$, $T(t)$, $Q(t)$, $K(t)$, and $C(t)$. To determine all these variables we require a seventh equation specifying the behavior of the capital stock. For golden ages—equilibria in which all variables change at constant relative rates—it is, given the other equations, necessary and sufficient that the ratio of capital to augmented labor be constant:

$$\frac{K(t)}{T(t)N(t)} = k. \qquad (7)$$

If we assume constant returns to scale in *(1)* then

$$Q(t) = T(t)N(t)F\left(\frac{K(t)}{T(t)N(t)}, 1\right), \qquad (8)$$

whence, by *(4)*, *(5)*, *(6)*, and *(7)*

$$\begin{aligned} Q(t) &= T(0)e^{\gamma t}N(0)e^{\gamma t}F(k, 1) \\ &= T(0)N(0)e^{2\gamma t}F(k, 1). \end{aligned} \qquad (9)$$

Hence, output will grow exponentially at the rate 2γ if the ratio of capital to augmented labor is fixed.

By virtue of *(4)*, *(5)*, *(6)*, and *(7)*, the capital stock will grow exponentially at the same rate:

$$K(t) = T(0)N(0)e^{2\gamma t}k. \qquad (10)$$

Therefore, investment will do the same:

$$\dot{K}(t) = 2\gamma T(0)N(0)e^{2\gamma t}k. \qquad (11)$$

Hence, by *(3)*, consumption will also grow at the rate 2γ and is given by

$$C(t) = [F(k, 1) - 2\gamma k]T(0)N(0)e^{2\gamma t}. \qquad (12)$$

For every k there corresponds a constant tangible investment-output ratio,

$$s = \frac{\dot{K}(t)}{Q(t)} = \frac{2\gamma k}{F(k, 1)}, \qquad (13)$$

and a constant marginal productivity of capital,

$$\frac{\partial Q(t)}{\partial K(t)} = F_K(k, 1). \qquad (14)$$

If capital receives its marginal product, therefore, its relative share of output will also be constant:

$$a = \frac{\partial Q(t)}{\partial K(t)} \frac{K(t)}{Q(t)} = \frac{F_K(k, 1)k}{F(k, 1)}. \qquad (15)$$

Thus constancy of the capital-augmented labor ratio together with *(1)* through *(6)* imply a golden age. Conversely, it can be shown that a golden age implies constancy of the ratio of capital to augmented labor.

That the golden-age or "natural" growth rate is simply 2γ is a striking result and one which suggests an empirical test of the model. But it is not likely that the model would perform well until the technology function is made to accommodate "imported" technical progress.

It has been shown that a golden age exists for every value of k and $R(0)$. Let us fix $R(0)$ and ask in which golden age—one golden age corresponds to every k—the path of consumption is maximal. In short, let us derive the Golden Rule of Accumulation in this model where technical progress is endogenous.

Assuming an interior maximum to be attained, we need merely differentiate $C(t)$ with respect to k in *(12)* and equate the derivative to zero:

$$F_K(k, 1) - 2\gamma = 0. \qquad (16)$$

Hence, the Golden Rule of Accumulation prescribes choosing k so as to equate the marginal productivity of capital to the golden-age rate of growth. Another way to express the Golden Rule of Accumulation results from multiplying both marginal productivity and growth rate by the capital-output ratio, whence

$$s = a. \qquad (17)$$

This states that, on the maximal consumption path, the investment-output ratio equals capital's competitive share. Or to put it another way, of the workers producing commodities, a proportion a of them earmark their output for investment along the maximal path.

This is the familiar rule. The endogeneity of technical progress does not alter the rule. Nor does it matter at which level we fix $R(0)$, provided only that $0 < R(0) < L_o$.

Let us now vary the ratio of researchers to commodity-producing workers, this time fixing the capital-augmented labor ratio and hence the tangible investment-output ratio. Corresponding to each value of $R(0)$ (and hence $N(0)$) is a different golden age and a certain consumption path. The higher $R(0)$ the greater will be the level of technology, $T(0)$, hence the greater will be output and consumption for any $N(0)$; but the higher $R(0)$ the smaller must $N(0)$ be, hence the smaller will output and consumption be for any given level of technology. It is immediately clear that neither $R(0) = L_o$ nor $R(0) = 0$ is consumption maximizing so that we may expect an interior maximum. What is the consumption-maximizing research level? That is, what is the Golden Rule of Research?

Looking again at *(12)*, we see that if we wish to maximize $C(t)$ we need only maximize "augmented labor," $T(0)N(0)$, subject to *(2)*. If this is surprising, note that since k and hence the tangible investment-output ratio is fixed, maximization of consumption is equivalent to maximization of output, $Q(t) = F(K(0), T(0)N(0))e^{2\gamma t}$; and that since $K(0) = kT(0)N(0)$ we are maximizing $F\bigl(kT(0)N(0),\, T(0)N(0)\bigr)$ which reduces to maximizing $T(0)N(0)$.

Differentiating $T(0)N(0)$ with respect to $R(0)$, subject to *(2)*, and equating the derivative to zero yields

$$0 = \frac{\partial T}{\partial R}\, N + \frac{\partial N}{\partial R}\, T \qquad (18)$$
$$= \eta N - T.$$

But from *(6)* we have $T(0) = \eta R(0)$ so that

$$N = R \qquad (19)$$

is the solution.[3] Thus we see that the Golden Rule of Research prescribes engaging exactly one half of the labor force in research. Note that just as the Golden Rule of Accumulation specifies that a fraction a of the commodity-producing workers should earmark their output for investment independently of the ratio of researchers to the labor force, the Golden Rule of Research specifies that one half the labor force should engage in research independently of the tangible-investment-output ratio or capital-augmented labor ratio.

Fifty percent is surprisingly large. My assumptions that the labor force is homogeneous and that no capital is required in research have biased the result toward high research. Later I shall relax both these assumptions.

It might be thought that our result would differ if we fixed not the tangible investment-output *ratio* or, equivalently, the capital-augmented labor *ratio* but rather the "absolute" path of the capital stock itself. But this is not so. Of course, we require exponential growth of capital at the rate 2γ for a golden age. So let us replace *(7)* by the condition

$$K(t) = K_o e^{2\gamma t}. \qquad (7a)$$

Then the golden-age consumption path, which is a function of $R(0)$, is

$$C(t) = F\bigl(K_o e^{2\gamma t},\, T(0)N(0)e^{2\gamma t}\bigr) - 2\gamma K_o e^{2\gamma t}$$
$$= [F\bigl(K_o,\, T(0)N(0)\bigr) - 2\gamma K_0]e^{2\gamma t}. \qquad (20)$$

---

[3] Or, in *(18)*, replace $\partial T/\partial R$ by T/R (by virtue of the proportionality between T and R) which yields $N/R = 1$.

We see that maximization of $C(t)$ with respect to $R(0)$ once again entails only the maximization of "augmented labor." It makes no difference whether we fix the "absolute" capital stock path or the path of the capital-augmented labor ratio (hence the tangible investment-output ratio).

The Golden Rule of Accumulation was expressed, among other ways, in terms of the marginal productivity of capital and the rate of growth. The former is the rate of return to investment in this model. Indeed, in more general models, it is always the rate of return which is equated to the growth rate along the Golden Rule path and not necessarily the marginal productivity of capital. The question may be asked, therefore, whether the Golden Rule of Research calls for equating the rate of return from research to the growth rate. We show now that it does.

To do this we cast the model into a discrete-time framework, where

$$C_t + I_t = Q_t, \ I_t = K_{t+1} - K_t. \tag{3a}$$

$$L_t = L_o(1 + \gamma)^t, \tag{4a}$$

$$R_t = R_0(1 + \gamma)^t, \tag{5a}$$

and

$$T_t = \Phi(R_{t-1}, R_{t-2}, \ldots) \tag{6a}$$

where

$$T_t = T_0(1 + \gamma)^t \quad \text{if } (5a) \text{ holds.}$$

Output can be expressed as follows:

$$Q_t = P(R_{t-1}, R_{t-2}, \ldots; I_{t-1}, I_{t-2}, \ldots; L_t - R_t). \tag{1a}$$

In a golden age where $Q_t = Q_0(1 + g)^t$ and $I_t = I_0(1 + g)^t$, we have

$$\begin{aligned}
Q_t = P\big(&R_t(1 + \gamma)^{-1}, R_t(1 + \gamma)^{-2}, \ldots; \\
&I_t(1 + g)^{-1}, I_t(1 + g)^{-2}, \ldots; \\
&L_t - R_t\big).
\end{aligned} \tag{9a}$$

Hence consumption in a golden age can be written

$$\begin{aligned}
C_t = P\big(&R_t(1 + \gamma)^{-1}, R_t(1 + \gamma)^{-2}, \ldots; \\
&I_t(1 + g)^{-1}, I_t(1 + g)^{-2}, \ldots; \\
&L_t - R_t\big) - I_t.
\end{aligned} \tag{12a}$$

As was demonstrated in the continuous time model, in a golden age Q_t, C_t, and I_t grow like $T_t N_t = T_0(1 + \gamma)^t N_0(1 + \gamma)^t$ so that $(1 + g) = (1 + \gamma)^2$.

As a preliminary exercise we show that (assuming an interior maximum) the Golden Rule of Accumulation prescribes equality of the rate of return from investment and the rate of growth: fix R_0 and maximize C_t with respect to I_t. This yields

$$\frac{\partial C_t}{\partial I_t} = 0 = \sum_1^\infty \frac{\partial P_t}{\partial I_{t-i}} (1 + g)^{-i} - 1$$

or

$$\sum_1^\infty \frac{\partial P_t}{\partial I_{t-i}} (1 + g)^{-i} = 1. \qquad (21)$$

Now we define the rate of return to investment at time t as that value of r such that

$$\sum_1^\infty \frac{\partial P_{t+i}}{\partial I_t} (1 + r)^{-i} = 1. \qquad (22)$$

Next we observe that in this nonvintage model, as well as in the vintage model, the marginal productivity at t of investment made at $t - i$ is equal to the marginal productivity at $t + i$ of investment at t *in a golden age*. (In fact, the model implies constancy of the marginal productivity of investment.) But if

$$\frac{\partial P_{t+i}}{\partial I_t} = \frac{\partial P_t}{\partial I_{t-i}}$$

then, by *(22)*,

$$\sum_1^\infty \frac{\partial P_t}{\partial I_{t-i}} (1 + r)^{-i} = 1. \qquad (23)$$

Equations *(21)* and *(23)* imply that $r = g$ when $\partial C_t/\partial I_t = 0$.

Let us now fix the investment path, that is, I_0, and maximize C_t with respect to R_t. This yields

$$\frac{\partial C_t}{\partial R_t} = 0 = \sum_1^\infty \frac{\partial P}{\partial R_{t-i}} (1 + \gamma)^{-i} - \frac{\partial P}{\partial N_t}$$

or

$$\sum_1^\infty \frac{\partial P}{\partial R_{t-i}} (1 + \gamma)^{-i} = \frac{\partial P}{\partial N_t}$$

or

$$\sum_1^\infty \frac{\partial P}{\partial R_{t-i}} \frac{\partial N_t}{\partial P} (1 + \gamma)^{-i} = 1. \qquad (24)$$

Note that the marginal productivity of labor i periods ago is

$$\left(\frac{\partial P}{\partial N}\right)_{t-i} = \frac{\partial P_t}{\partial N_t} (1 + \gamma)^{-i} \quad \text{or}$$

$$\frac{\partial N_t}{\partial P_t} = \left(\frac{\partial N}{\partial P}\right)_{t-i} (1 + \gamma)^{-i}, \qquad (25)$$

since the average and marginal productivity of labor is growing like $(1 + \gamma)^t$ in a golden age. Thus we may write

$$\sum_1^\infty \left[\frac{\partial P_t}{\partial R_{t-i}} \left(\frac{\partial N}{\partial P}\right)_{t-i}\right] [(1 + \gamma)^2]^{-i} = 1. \qquad (26)$$

The expression in the first bracket measures the increase in product at time t resulting from the sacrifice of one unit of output at time $t - i$ in order to release some commodity-producing workers into research. It is $-(\partial P_t/\partial P_{t-i})$ or what may be called the marginal productivity at time t of "investment in technology" at time $t - i$.

Analogously to the previous exercise we observe now that *in a golden age* the marginal productivity at time $t + i$ of investment in technology at time t is equal to the marginal productivity at t of investment in technology at time $t - i$. This stationarity of the current marginal productivity of investment in technology i periods earlier follows from the constancy of the input proportions in both the production and technology functions.[4] Thus if the rate of return to investment in technology at time t is defined by

$$\sum_1^\infty \frac{-\partial P_{t+i}}{\partial P_t} (1 + r)^{-i} = 1, \qquad (27)$$

where

$$\frac{-\partial P_{t+i}}{\partial P_t} = \frac{\partial P_{t+i}}{\partial R_t} \frac{\partial N_t}{\partial P_t}$$

and denotes the marginal productivity at $t + i$ of investment in technology at t, then, by our stationarity assumption, we may

[4] Constancy over time of $-(\partial P_t/\partial P_{t-i})$ is due to the fact that $(\partial N/\partial P)_{t-i}$ declines geometrically at rate γ due to productivity growth while $\partial P_t/\partial R_{t-i}$ increases at rate γ due to the growth of $N(t)$ at that rate.

also write

$$\sum_{1}^{\infty} \frac{-\partial P_t}{\partial P_{t-i}} (1 + r)^{-i} = 1. \qquad (28)$$

Equations *(26)* and *(28)* imply that, when $\partial C_t/\partial R_t = 0, 1 + r = (1 + \gamma)^2$; but $(1 + \gamma)^2 = 1 + g$ so that $r = g$. Thus the Golden Rule of Research prescribes equating the rate of return from investment in technology to the rate of growth.

We have been maximizing golden-age consumption with respect to research effort while holding constant the capital stock or the ratio of capital to augmented labor; and maximizing golden-age consumption with respect to capital intensity while holding research effort constant. It is perfectly clear that if we wish to maximize golden-age consumption with respect both to capital intensity and research effort we must equate the rate of return of both investment in technology and investment in tangible capital to the rate of growth. We may call this truly maximal consumption path *the* Golden Rule path. This Golden Rule path is *dynamically efficient*: like some but not all golden-age paths, the rates of return to the two kinds of investment are equal; equality of the rates of return is clearly one necessary condition for dynamical efficiency. And, secondly, this common rate of return—which is the rate of return to saving—is not smaller than the rate of growth.

In the particular, highly simple model we have been analyzing, exactly $\frac{1}{2}L(t)$ workers will produce commodities in this Golden Rule state while $\frac{1}{2}aL(t)$ workers will earmark their commodity output for investment. But these characteristics, unlike the equalities pertaining to rates of return, are due to the critical assumptions that the labor force is homogenous and that capital is unproductive in the research sector. I now relax these assumptions.

A Nonhomogenous Labor Force   I shall continue to suppose, as an approximation, that no worker has an absolute advantage in the production of commodities. But I suppose now that all workers differ in their effectiveness in research. If we require just one researcher, then, for efficiency, we must assign that worker with the greatest comparative, and hence absolute, advantage in research. If we require an additional worker we assign that worker with the next greatest absolute advantage; but the increase of "effective research" will not be proportional because the second worker is inferior to the first. Thus I suppose that, with efficient allocation of labor, "effective research" increases with the number of researchers at a decreasing rate; we take as fixed here the size of the labor force.

Second, I suppose that the skill mix is in some sense stationary over time in that if both the labor force and the number of researchers required is doubled, we can, by suitable assignment of workers, double effective research.

Third, I suppose that without research there is no effective research.

To express these assumptions mathematically I replace $R(v)$ by the "effective research function," $E(R(v), L(v))$, in the technology function,

$$T(t) = \int_{-\infty}^{t} H(E(R(v)L(v)), T(v - \omega)) \, dv, \qquad (29)$$

imposing on the effective research function the following restrictions:

$$E_R(R(v), L(v)) > 0, E_{RR}(R(v), L(v)) < 0 \qquad (a)$$

$$E(R(v), L(v)) = L(v)E\left(\frac{R(v)}{L(v)}, 1\right) \qquad (b)$$

$$E(0, L(v)) = 0. \qquad (c)$$

I suppose, as before, that $H(E, T)$ is homogenous of degree one; i.e., a doubling of effective research at v and of technology at $v - \omega$ will cause a doubling of the absolute rate of increase of technology at v, $\dot{T}(v) = H(E(R(v), L(v)), T(v - \omega))$. And, as before, I suppose that $H(0, T) = 0$.

It is now easy to see that in a golden age, in which $R(t)$ and $L(t)$ both grow exponentially at rate γ, the technology path will also grow exponentially at rate γ and will satisfy the transcendental equation, analogous to (e''),

$$\gamma = e^{-\gamma\omega}h\left(\frac{E(R(0), L_o)}{T(0)} e^{\gamma\omega}\right). \qquad (30)$$

Thus the golden-age "level" of technology is proportional to "effective research," so that we obtain

$$T(t) = \beta E(R(0), L_o)e^{\lambda t}. \qquad (31)$$

To maximize golden-age consumption with respect to research effort, it suffices, as before, to maximize "augmented labor" subject to the constraint [in *(2)*] $R(0) + N(0) = L_o$. Equating to zero the derivative of $T(0)N(0)$ with respect to $R(0)$ yields

$$0 = \frac{\partial T(0)}{\partial R(0)} N(0) + \frac{\partial N(0)}{\partial R(0)} T(0)$$

$$= \eta \frac{\partial E}{\partial R} N(0) - T(0) \qquad \text{[by (2) and (31)]} \qquad (32)$$

$$= \eta \frac{\partial E}{\partial R} N(0) - \eta E(R(0), L_o). \quad \text{[by (31)]}$$

This equation can be written in the form

$$\frac{R(0)}{N(0)} = \frac{\partial E(R(0), L_o)/\partial R(0)}{E(R(0), L_o)/R(0)}. \qquad (33)$$

The right-hand side of *(33)* is the elasticity of effective research with respect to research. (It is stationary over time for fixed R/L.) Thus the Golden Rule of Research prescribes equating the ratio of researchers to nonresearchers to the research elasticity of effective research. If E were proportional to R, as we supposed in the first part of this paper, this elasticity would be unitary; then $R/N = 1$ which was the result obtained before. But on our new assumptions on $E(R, L)$ this elasticity is unitary only at $R = 0$; on our assumption that $E_{RR} < 0$ this elasticity must be smaller than one for all $R > 0$. Hence, as R/N is increased toward one, there must come a point, $(\widehat{R/N})$, where *(33)* is satisfied. Clearly, $(\widehat{R/N}) < 1$ since $(\widehat{R/N})$ could equal one only if the elasticity equaled one at $R = \frac{1}{2}L$ which is impossible for $L > 0$. Thus we see that if workers have differing absolute advantage in research but are equally productive in the commodity-producing sector, the Golden Rule of Research dictates assigning less than half of all workers to the research sector.

Capital in the Research Sector   Heretofore I have supposed that capital could not contribute to research effort. Let us suppose now that it can and that, as seems reasonable, "effective research" is homogenous of degree one in $R(t)$, $L(t)$, and $M(t)$ where $M(t)$ denotes the stock of capital employed in the research sector:

$$T(t) = \int_{-\infty}^{t} H\big(E(R(v), L(v), M(v)), T(v - \omega)\big)\, dv \quad (34)$$

where

$$E_R > 0, \ E_{RR} < 0, \ E_M > 0, \ E_{MM} < 0. \quad (a)$$

$$E = L\, E\left(\frac{R}{L}, 1, \frac{M}{L}\right) = M\, E\left(\frac{R}{M}, \frac{L}{M}, 1\right) \quad (b)$$

$$E(0, L, M) = E(R, L, 0) = 0. \quad (c)$$

As before, I suppose that $H(E, T)$ is homogenous of degree one in E and T and that $E(0, T) = 0$.

From *(34)* we have

$$\frac{\dot{T}(t)}{T(t)} = \frac{T(t - \omega)}{T(t)}\, H\left(\frac{E\big(R(t), L(t), M(t)\big)}{T(t - \omega)}, 1\right). \quad (35)$$

Hence, if the technology grows exponentially and has always done so it must be that "effective research" also grows exponentially at the same rate, say j, so as to satisfy *(35)*:

$$j = e^{-j\omega} H\left(\frac{E\big(R(0), L_o, M(0)\big)e^{jt}}{T(0)e^{j(t-\omega)}}, 1\right)$$

$$= e^{-j\omega} H\left(\frac{E\big(R(0), L_o, M(0)\big)}{T(0)}\, e^{j\omega}, 1\right). \quad (36)$$

Now effective research would indeed grow exponentially if $R(t)$, $L(t)$, and $M(t)$ all grew at the same rate j. Then "augmented labor" in the commodity-producing sector would, in a golden age, grow at the rate $j + \gamma = 2j$ since $R(t)$ and $N(t)$ must grow at the same rate. But then capital in the commodity sector would have to grow at the rate $2j$. But $M(t)$ grows only at the rate j so that the two capital stocks would not grow at the same rate; therefore total capital would not grow exponentially, nor would investment and therefore consumption. So a golden age is impossible if $R(t)$, $L(t)$, and $M(t)$ grow at the same rate.

But if $R(t)$, $L(t)$, and $M(t)$ grow at different rates $\big(M(t)$ growing like $j + \gamma\big)$ then can $E(R, L, M)$ grow exponentially? The answer is no unless "effective research" is a Cobb-Douglas function. Let us assume it is. Then if both $R(t)$ and $L(t)$ grow at rate γ and $M(t)$ grows at rate m the relative rate of growth of "effective research," and hence of the technology, j, will be given by

$$j = \alpha m + (\beta' + \beta'')\gamma \qquad (\textit{37})$$

where α is the capital elasticity of "effective research" and β' and β'' are the elasticities of effective research with respect to $R(t)$ and $L(t)$ respectively. By the homogeneity postulate, $\beta' + \beta'' = 1 - \alpha$.

Now "augmented labor" will, in a golden age, grow at rate $j + \gamma$ so that the rate of growth of output and capital in the commodity sector, say g, must also be $j + \gamma$. Hence

$$g = \alpha m + (1 - \alpha)\gamma + \gamma. \qquad (\textit{38})$$

But, for a golden age, capital must grow at the same rate in both sectors, otherwise total capital cannot grow exponentially. Hence, substituting

$$g = m \qquad (\textit{39})$$

into *(38)* we obtain

$$g = \frac{(2 - \alpha)\gamma}{1 - \alpha} \qquad (\textit{40})$$

as the golden-age growth rate of capital in both sectors and of output. In the special case in which capital is unproductive, so that $\alpha = 0$, we obtain once again the result that $g = 2\gamma$. But if $\alpha > 0$, $g > 2\gamma$. Since capital grows faster than labor, by virtue of technical progress, it is helpful to the technical progress rate, and hence the growth rate, that capital can be employed in the research sector. For $g > \gamma$ so that when $m = g$, $j = \alpha m + (1 - \alpha)\gamma$ exceeds γ for all $\alpha > 0$.

I turn now to the question of how the productivity of capital in research affects the proportion of the labor force and the proportion of the capital stock engaged in research on the Golden Rule path. First, given that total capital has been allocated between the research and commodity sectors in a consumption-maximizing way, how must labor be allocated on the Golden Rule path? As before, labor is allocated on the Golden Rule path so as to maximize "augmented labor" in the commodity sector. Thus $T(0)N(0)$ is at a maximum with respect to $R(0)$. Hence

$$0 = \frac{\partial T(0)}{\partial R(0)} N(0) + \frac{\partial N(0)}{\partial R(0)} T(0) \qquad (41)$$

$$= \eta \frac{\partial E(R(0), L_o, M(0))}{\partial R(0)} N(0) - T(0).$$

But

$$T(t) = \eta \, E(R(0), L_o, M(0)) \, e^{[\alpha g + (1-\alpha)\gamma]t}. \qquad (42)$$

Therefore

$$\frac{R(0)}{N(0)} = \frac{\partial E(R(0), L_o, M(0))/\partial R(0)}{E(R(0), L_o, M(0))/R(0)} = \beta'. \qquad (43)$$

Once again we find that the ratio of researchers to nonresearchers equals the elasticity of effective research with respect to researchers. In the present Cobb-Douglas case, this elasticity is the constant β', which is less than one by our homogeneity assumption.

We see that the presence of capital in the effective research function is another reason why less than half the labor force is assigned to research on the Golden Rule path. For even if the labor force is homogeneous ($\beta'' = 0$), the elasticity of effective research with respect to the number of researchers, β', must be less than one if capital is productive ($\alpha > 0$) and there are constant returns to scale in effective research ($\alpha + \beta' = 1$).

What of the allocation of total capital between the research and commodity sectors on the Golden Rule path? Given the exponentially increasing path of total capital and the allocation of labor appropriate to the Golden Rule path, that part of total capital allocated to the commodity sector, $K(0)$, is such as to maximize

$$C(t) = \{F(K(0), T(0) N(0)) - (\dot{K}(0) + \dot{M}(0))\} e^{gt} \qquad (44)$$

on the Golden Rule path. Hence, equating to zero the derivative of

$C(t)$ with respect to $K(0)$ and noting that $dM/dK = -1$ we obtain

$$0 = F_K + F_N N(0) \frac{dT(0)}{dK}$$

$$= F_K - F_N N(0) \eta \frac{\partial E(R(0), L_o, M(0))}{\partial M(0)}$$

$$= \left(\frac{F_K K(0)}{Q(0)} \right) - \frac{K(0)}{T(0)} \left(\frac{T(0) F_N N(0)}{Q} \right) \eta \frac{\partial E}{\partial M} \quad (45)$$

$$= (a) - \frac{K}{\eta E} (b) \eta \frac{\partial E}{\partial M}$$

$$= \frac{a}{b} - \frac{K}{M} \frac{\partial E / \partial M}{E / M},$$

whence

$$\frac{M(0)}{K(0)} = \frac{b}{a} \frac{\partial E(R(0), L_o, M(0))/\partial M(0)}{E(R(0), L_o, M(0))/M(0)} = \frac{1-a}{a} \alpha. \quad (46)$$

On the Golden Rule path, therefore, the ratio of capital in research to capital in the commodity sector depends not only on the capital elasticity of effective research but also upon a, the capital elasticity of output. Note that $M(0) = 0$ if $\alpha = 0$. Note too that the research sector will be more capital intensive than the commodity sector—that is, $M/K > R/N$—if and only if $(b/a)\alpha > \beta'$ or $\alpha/\beta' > a/b$ which was to be expected.

Other theorems which could be established are that, in the present model as well as in the model where capital is unproductive in the research sector, the rates of return to investment in technology and to investment in the commodity sector are equal to the rate of growth on the Golden Rule path. Proofs of these theorems would be essentially a repetition of proofs given earlier.

CONCLUDING REMARKS

I postulated a certain technology function which is conducive to golden ages. It was shown that when golden-age consumption is maximal with respect to research effort, the rate of return to "investment in technology" equals the rate of growth. I called this equalization the Golden Rule of Research. It was also shown that when golden-age consumption is maximized with respect to tangible investment in the commodity sector, the rate of return from tangible investment equals the rate of growth. This is the familiar Golden Rule of Accumulation. When golden-age consumption is maximal with respect to both kinds of investment, the two rates of return are therefore both equal to each other and to the rate of growth. This suggests the General Golden Rule of Investment: to maximize golden-age consumption, assuming an interior maximum to exist, equate the rate of return from each kind of investment to the rate of growth.

I also characterized the Golden Rule state in terms of labor allocation. It was shown that if the labor force is homogeneous and capital is unproductive in the research sector then exactly one half the labor force is assigned to research on the Golden Rule path. But if capital is productive in research or if the skill at research of the marginal researcher falls with increasing numbers of researchers, due to a nonhomogeneous skill mix, then, on certain assumptions, less then one half of the labor force does research on the Golden Rule path.

Investment in Humans, Technological Diffusion, and the Golden Rule of Education

----

A recent paper by Richard Nelson and the present author[1] advanced the hypothesis that education increases the pace of technological diffusion. After a condensed restatement of the hypothesis and underlying theory presented in that paper, I shall develop a complete model of education, diffusion, and growth, based on a diffusion model presented in the earlier paper, and derive from it a Golden Rule of Education.

THE HYPOTHESIS

A basic principle in the theory of the relation between education and economic growth is that certain kinds of education equip a man to perform certain jobs or functions, or enable a man to perform a given function more effectively. Thus far, growth theorists have applied this principle only to completely routinized jobs, jobs which require no adaptation to change or learning in the performance of the job. (Even a highly routinized job may require education to master the necessary skills.) In its usual, rather general form, the theory postulates a production function

[1] R. R. Nelson and E. S. Phelps, "Investment in Humans, Technological Diffusion and Economic Growth," *American Economic Review*, Vol. 56 (May 1966), pp. 69–75.

that states how maximum current output depends upon the current services of tangible capital goods, the current number of men performing each of these jobs, possibly the current educational attainment of each of these job holders, and possibly time. Such a production function implies that the marginal productivity of education can, for given inputs, remain positive forever even if the technology is stationary.

But education is also important to the performance of functions which require adaptation to change. The function of innovating is a prime example. It is a reasonable hypothesis that the more educated are those in production management, the quicker they will be to introduce new processes and products. To put the hypothesis simply, educated people make good innovators, so that education speeds the process of technological diffusion.

There is evidence for this hypothesis in United States agriculture. Relatively well-educated farmers have tended to adopt productive innovations earlier than farmers with relatively little education. Undoubtedly part of the explanation is that the greater schooling of the better-educated farmers has increased their ability to read and understand the information on new processes and products disseminated by governments, farm journals, seed and equipment companies, and so on. With this technical information in hand, the more-educated farmer is better able to discriminate between promising and unpromising ideas and is hence less likely to make mistakes. The less-educated farmer, for whom the information in technical literature means less, is prudent to delay the introduction of a new technique until he has concrete, practical evidence of its profitability.

A specific model of education, diffusion, and growth will now be developed.

THE MODEL

I shall work with a simple model in which there is an aggregate production function. Technical progress is postulated to be Harrod neutral everywhere so that it can be described as purely labor augmenting. If we let Q denote output, K denote capital, N denote labor in production, and t denote time, our production function takes the form

$$Q(t) = F[K(t), A(t)N(t)]. \qquad (1)$$

Constant returns to scale is postulated.

It is now possible to speak meaningfully about the "level" or "index" of technology. In particular, $A(t)$ is our index of *technology in practice*. Undoubtedly it would be more realistic to work with a vintage model of production in which $A(t)$ is the *best-practice* level of technology, the average technology level embodied in the latest capital goods actually being produced. But the present nonvintage model will serve adequately to indicate the main points I wish to make.

In addition to the *practiced* level of technology, I introduce the notion of the *theoretical* level of technology. This is defined as the level of technology in practice that would exist if technological diffusion were complete and instantaneous. It is a measure of the stock of knowledge or body of production techniques that is available to innovators. I shall suppose that the theoretical technology level advances exogenously at a constant exponential rate λ:

$$T(t) = T_o e^{\lambda t}, \quad \lambda > 0. \qquad (2)$$

Turning to the diffusion hypothesis, I postulate that the rate of increase of the level of technology in practice is an increasing function of some index of *per capita* educational attainment, h, and of the gap between the theoretical technology level and the technology level in practice. Specifically,

$$\dot{A}(t) = \Phi(h)[T(t) - A(t)] \qquad (3)$$

or equivalently

$$\frac{\dot{A}(t)}{A(t)} = \Phi(h)\left[\frac{T(t) - A(t)}{A(t)}\right], \quad \Phi(0) = 0, \ \Phi'(h) > 0. \qquad (3a)$$

The quantity $(T(t) - A(t))/A(t)$ will be called the "gap."

If h is constant, some interesting results follow. One result is that, for positive h, the rate of increase of the level of technology in practice, $\dot{A}(t)/A(t)$, will settle down to the value λ in the long run, independently of the level of h. The reason is that if, say, h

is sufficiently large that $\dot{A}(t)/A(t) > \lambda$ initially, then the gap narrows; but the narrowing of the gap reduces $\dot{A}(t)/A(t)$; the gap continues to narrow until, in the limit, $\dot{A}(t)/A(t)$ has fallen to the value λ at which point the system is in equilibrium with a constant gap.

Nevertheless h makes a difference. The asymptotic or equilibrium path of $A(t)$, say $A^*(t)$, is an increasing function of h. There is an analogy here with those models of growth which make the long-run rate of output growth independent of the saving ratio, though the long-run "level" of output depends upon the magnitude of the saving ratio.

These results are confirmed by the solution, in *(4)*, of the differential equation obtained by substituting *(2)* into *(3)*:

$$A(t) = \left(A_o - \frac{\Phi}{\Phi + \lambda} \, T_o \right) e^{-\Phi t} + \frac{\Phi}{\Phi + \lambda} \, T_o e^{\lambda t}. \quad (4)$$

As *(4)* shows, the equilibrium path, $A^*(t)$, is

$$A^*(t) = \frac{\Phi(h)}{\Phi(h) + \lambda} \, T_o e^{\lambda t}. \quad (5)$$

An interesting property of this relation is that the elasticity of $A^*(t)$ with respect to h is increasing in λ:

$$\frac{\partial A^*(t)}{\partial h} \, \frac{h}{A^*(t)} = \left[\frac{h \Phi'(h)}{\Phi(h)} \right] \left[\frac{\lambda}{\Phi(h) + \lambda} \right]. \quad (6)$$

This indicates that the effectiveness of increased educational attainment is greater the more technologically dynamic is the economy. It suggests the possibility that society will want to invest more in education relative to tangible capital the more dynamic the technology. This is further suggested by later results.

To complete the model, I introduce the following additional relations and variables. The number of educators, E, plus the number of students, S, plus the number of production workers, N, comprise the total labor force, L:

$$E(t) + S(t) + N(t) = L(t). \quad (7)$$

The labor force and its components all grow exponentially over time at rate $\gamma > 0$. Hence

$$L(t) = L_o e^{\gamma t} \qquad (8)$$

$$\frac{E(t)}{L(t)} = b = \text{constant}. \qquad (9)$$

$$\frac{S(t)}{L(t)} = s = \text{constant}. \qquad (10)$$

$$\frac{N(t)}{L(t)} = n = \text{constant}. \qquad (11)$$

In this state of balanced labor-force growth, the index of *per capita* educational attainment, h, of every post-education individual is assumed to be an increasing function of both b and s:

$$h = \psi(b, s), \quad \psi_1 > 0, \ \psi_2 > 0 \\ \psi(0, 0) = 0. \qquad (12)$$

I interpret this model as one in which everyone attends school for some (equal) length of time; an increase in s connotes a longer period of education since it is the number of students (expressed as a proportion of the labor force) attending school at any moment of time.

Finally, I postulate golden-age growth: the ratio of capital to "augmented" or "effective" labor in production is a constant, k; since N grows exponentially at rate γ and, in equilibrium, $A(t)$ grows exponentially at rate λ, as indicated by *(5)*, we have

$$\frac{K(t)}{A^*(t)N(t)} = \frac{K(t)}{A^*(0)e^{\lambda t}N(0)e^{\gamma t}} = \frac{K(t)}{A^*(0)N(0)e^{gt}} = k, \qquad (13)$$
$$g = \lambda + \gamma.$$

The following expressions for golden-age consumption, $C(t)$, can then be obtained:

$$C(t) = F[K(t), A^*(t)N(t)] - \dot{K}(t) \\ = F[kA^*(0)N(0)e^{gt}, A^*(0)N(0)e^{gt}] - gK(t) \qquad (14) \\ = [F(k, 1) - gk]A^*(0)N(0)e^{gt},$$

the last result by virtue of constant returns to scale.

THE GOLDEN RULE OF EDUCATION

To find the value of $N(0)$ or n which maximizes golden-age consumption it appears that we need merely maximize $A^*(0)N(0)$ with respect to $N(0)$. But we first need to determine b and s as functions of n since h and hence $A^*(0)$ is not simply a function of the sum $b + s$.

For efficiency in the education sector, b and s must be such as to maximize h for given n. Hence it is necessary to maximize

$$h = \psi(b, 1 - b - n) \qquad (15)$$

subject to a constant n. Equating to zero the derivative of h with respect to b we obtain

$$\psi_1(b, 1 - b - n) - \psi_2(b, 1 - b - n) = 0. \qquad (16)$$

It will be assumed that *(16)* gives a unique interior maximum with $b > 0$, $s = 1 - b - n > 0$. The second order condition, *(17)*, is therefore assumed to be satisfied:

$$\psi_{11} - \psi_{12} - \psi_{21} + \psi_{22} < 0. \qquad (17)$$

This implies a diminishing marginal rate of substitution between faculty and students.

Taking the total differential of *(16)* we obtain

$$\frac{db}{dn} = \frac{dE}{dN} = \frac{\psi_{12} - \psi_{22}}{\psi_{11} - \psi_{12} - \psi_{21} + \psi_{22}}. \qquad (18)$$

It is reasonable to suppose that $\psi_{12} > 0$ and $\psi_{22} < 0$ so that $db/dn < 0$, but in any case, $E(0)$ is a single-valued function of $N(0)$.

Now we can proceed to maximize $A^*(0)N(0)$ to find the consumption-maximizing golden-age path (for any given k). The problem is to maximize

$$A^*(0)N(0) = \frac{\Phi\left[\psi\left(\frac{E}{L}, 1 - \frac{E}{L} - \frac{N}{L}\right)\right] T_o N(0)}{\Phi\left[\psi\left(\frac{E}{L}, 1 - \frac{E}{L} - \frac{N}{L}\right)\right] + \lambda} \qquad (19)$$

with respect to $N(0)$.

The total derivative of $A^*(0)N(0)$ with respect to $N(0)$ is

$$
\begin{aligned}
\frac{d(A^*N)}{dN} &= \frac{dA^*}{dN} N + A^* \\
&= \left(\frac{dA^*}{dh}\right)\left(\frac{dh}{dN}\right) N + A^* \\
&= \left\{ T_o \left[\frac{(\Phi + \lambda)\Phi' - \Phi\Phi'}{(\Phi + \lambda)^2} \right] \right\} \times \\
& \quad \left\{ \left(\frac{\psi_1}{L} - \frac{\psi_2}{L}\right) \frac{dE}{dN} - \frac{\psi_2}{L} \right\} N + \frac{\Phi}{\Phi + \lambda} T_o.
\end{aligned}
\tag{20}
$$

Equating this derivative to zero and noting that, for efficiency, $\psi_1 - \psi_2 = 0$ as shown in *(16)*, we obtain the necessary condition for an interior maximum:

$$
-\left\{ \frac{\lambda\Phi'[\psi(b, 1 - b - n)]\psi_2(b, 1 - b - n)}{\Phi[\psi(b, 1 - b - n)] + \lambda} \right\} n \tag{21}
$$
$$
+ \Phi[\psi(b, 1 - b - n)] = 0.
$$

This may be written

$$
n = \frac{(\Phi + \lambda)\Phi}{\lambda\Phi'\psi_2}. \tag{21a}
$$

Since b is a function of n, independently of λ, *(21)* is of the form

$$
-H(n, \lambda)n + J(n) = 0. \tag{21b}
$$

In these terms, the second-order condition that the stationary value be a maximum is

$$
-H_n(n, \lambda)n - H(n, \lambda) + J'(n) < 0. \tag{22}
$$

I omit expression of this condition in terms of the original functions. It can be stated that this condition is easily satisfied under reasonable assumptions on those functions.

I shall assume that a unique interior (local) maximum exists. (Of course, $n = 0$ and $n = 1$ could not be maxima since, for those values of n, $A^*(0)N(0) = 0$.) Hence *(16)*, *(21)*, and *(22)* characterize uniquely the consumption-maximizing golden-age or Golden Rule path.

It was seen earlier that the elasticity of A^* with respect to h is increasing in λ. This suggested the hypothesis that more resources ought to be devoted to the education sector the more dynamic is the technology. Hence it is natural to ask whether the Golden Rule value of n is decreasing in λ in this model.

Differentiating *(21b)* totally, we obtain

$$\frac{dn}{d\lambda} = \frac{H_\lambda(n, \lambda)n}{-H_n(n, \lambda)n - H(n, \lambda) + J'(n)}. \qquad (23)$$

Since the second-order condition *(22)* is satisfied (by virtue of the assumption that a Golden Rule path exists), the denominator in *(23)* is negative. The numerator is positive since $n > 0$ and $\partial H / \partial \lambda > 0$ (as can be seen from *(21)*). Hence $dn/d\lambda$ is negative, as conjectured.

As for the effect of an increase of λ on Golden Rule *tangible* capital intensity, $\hat{k}$, where $f'(\hat{k}) = \lambda + \gamma$ defines $\hat{k}$, one can see that $\hat{k}$ will fall if and only if $f''(k) < 0$ (diminishing returns). The Golden Rule tangible investment-output ratio, $\hat{s} = f'(\hat{k})\hat{k}/f(\hat{k})$, will also fall (with $\hat{k}$) if the substitution elasticity exceeds one, and rise if the elasticity is less than one. Thus an increase of λ may or may not entail a rise of tangible investment.

CONCLUDING REMARKS

A model of economic growth has been constructed which emphasizes the role of education in speeding technological diffusion and hence, in the long run, increasing the "level" of the technology in practice. As was shown, it is reasonable to expect a Golden Rule of Education to exist in this model. It was demonstrated that if a Golden Rule path exists, Golden Rule growth will require more resources in education the more technologically progressive is the economy.

On the Feasibility of Targeted
Growth through Personal
Income Taxation and the Social
Virtue of Private Thrift

More than twenty years have passed since the publication of
Evsey Domar's classic paper, "The 'Burden of the Debt' and the
National Income."[1] That paper dispelled the fears of many that
an economy which supported aggregate demand by means of a
budgetary deficit would eventually sink under the weight of the
taxes necessary to service the rapidly rising public debt. Domar
showed that if the deficit required for full employment is proportional to the national income and the full-employment income
grows at a constant relative rate then the debt as a ratio to national
income will approach a finite limit; and if, further, the interest
rate is constant then so too will the debt service as a ratio to
income. Moreover, if interest on the public debt is a part (but not
the whole) of "taxable income" then the debt service as a ratio to
taxable income will approach a limit which is less than 100 percent.

However, the behavior of the tax rate, as distinct from the
debt service-income ratio, was neglected by Domar. This note
repairs that omission and proceeds to study the feasibility and
determinants of the income tax rate and the proportionate algebraic deficit required to maintain the economy on the targeted
full-employment path. Some consequences of a change of private

[1] *American Economic Review*, Vol. 34 (December 1944), pp. 798–827. Reprinted in *Readings in Fiscal Policy* (Irwin, 1955), pp. 479–502, and with a
new foreword, in E. D. Domar, *Essays in the Theory of Economic Growth*
(Oxford, 1957), pp. 35–69.

thrift in a controlled economy are also examined. Our chief findings are described at the conclusion of the paper.

THE MODEL

In the spirit of the Domar paper I postulate the following:

1. There is a full-employment path of money national income, $\overline{Y}_t$, (possibly the only full-employment path or one among many) having the property of a constant rate of growth, λ:

$$\overline{Y}_t = \overline{Y}_o e^{\lambda t}. \qquad (1)$$

To insure that actual income, Y_t, takes this path is the objective of fiscal and monetary policies.

2. To realize this income path, investment expenditures must be some constant proportion, k, of targeted income:

$$I_t = k\overline{Y}_t. \qquad (2)$$

3. Associated with this path is a constant rate of interest, ι, which the government pays on the public debt. This is the interest rate that the monetary authorities find necessary to bring about the required path of investment demand.

4. Desired government expenditures, $\overline{G}_t$, are a constant proportion, γ, of targeted national income, and desired noninterest transfer payments by government, B_t, ("benefits") are a constant proportion, β, of targeted income:

$$\overline{G}_t = \gamma \overline{Y}_t \qquad (3)$$

$$\overline{B}_t = \beta \overline{Y}_t. \qquad (4)$$

I assume that $\gamma + k < 1$ so that resources are left for private consumption.

5. Private consumption expenditure demand is a constant proportion, π, of disposable income. Letting D_t denote the debt, T_t taxes, and Y_t actual money income:

$$C_t = \pi(Y_t + \iota D_t + B_t - T_t), \quad 0 < \pi \leq 1. \qquad (5)$$

6. Taxes are proportional to taxable income, $Y_t + \iota D_t$, τ_t being the proportional tax rate:

$$T_t = \tau_t(Y_t + \iota D_t). \qquad (6)$$

7. Any shortfall between taxes and government outlays is financed by the issue of interest-bearing debt. Hence the rate of change of the debt, $\dot{D}_t \equiv dD_t/dt$, equals the "deficit":

$$\dot{D}_t = (\gamma + \beta)Y_t + \iota D_t - \tau_t(Y_t + \iota D_t). \qquad (7)$$

If the target national income is to be realized then, by virtue of the income identity $C_t = Y_t - I_t - G_t$, the required consumption expenditure at time t, $\overline{C}_t$, is

$$\overline{C}_t = \overline{Y}_t(1 - k - \gamma). \qquad (8)$$

Equations (5) and (8) imply what disposable income must be in order that consumption demand meet the requirement. Using the budget identity, $T_t + a_t Y_t = (\gamma + \beta)Y_t + \iota D_t$ where a_t denotes the deficit as a proportion of national income, we can express disposable income in terms of a_t, Y_t, and γ:

$$Y_t + \iota D_t + B_t - T_t = Y_t(1 + a_t - \gamma) \qquad (9)$$

whence, by (5),

$$C_t = \pi(1 + a_t - \gamma)Y_t. \qquad (10)$$

Therefore if $\overline{Y}_t$ is to be realized, meaning $Y_t = \overline{Y}_t$ and $C_t = \overline{C}_t$, then a_t must satisfy the equation, derived from (8) and (10),

$$\pi(1 + a_t - \gamma) = 1 - \gamma - k.$$

or

$$a = \frac{(1 - \pi)(1 - \gamma) - k}{\pi}. \qquad (11)$$

As Domar knew, the required proportionate deficit is constant over time. It will be positive if π, γ, and k are small. As π approaches unity, a approaches $-k$; as π approaches zero, a increases without limit. However for every π, $0 < \pi \leq 1$, there is an a, $-k < a < \infty$, that will satisfy (11).

Recognizing that the proportionate deficit is constant over time we can write

$$\dot{D}_t = a\overline{Y}_t, \quad a = \text{constant.} \qquad (12)$$

Finally, we can derive from the budget equation (7) the required tax rate at time t, as a function of $\overline{Y}_t$, D_t and the required a:

$$\tau_t = \frac{\iota D_t}{\overline{Y}_t + \iota D_t} + \frac{(\gamma + \beta - a)\overline{Y}_t}{\overline{Y}_t + \iota D_t}. \qquad (13)$$

The tax rate will have to be revised continuously if $D_t/\overline{Y}_t$ changes over time.

DOMAR'S RESULTS

Domar showed that if $a > 0$ a kind of steady state is approached (if the initial state is different from it) in which $D_t/\overline{Y}_t$ and $\iota D_t/(\overline{Y}_t + \iota D_t)$ are constant. To prove this he substituted *(1)* in *(12)* to obtain the differential equation (writing Y_t in place of $\overline{Y}_t$ for neatness):

$$\dot{D}_t = aY_o e^{\lambda t}, \qquad (14)$$

the solution of which is

$$D_t = D_o + \frac{a}{\lambda} Y_o(e^{\lambda t} - 1) \qquad (15)$$

where D_o is the (initial) amount of debt at $t = 0$. It is immediately clear that the debt tends eventually to grow at the rate λ, no faster than output. From *(15)* we obtain

$$\frac{D_t}{Y_t} = \frac{D_o}{Y_o} e^{-\lambda t} + \frac{a}{\lambda} - \frac{a}{\lambda} e^{-\lambda t}. \qquad (16)$$

Hence

$$\lim_{t \to \infty} \frac{D_t}{Y_t} = \frac{a}{\lambda}. \qquad (17)$$

As a matter of notation, let the limiting value of any variable, x_t, be denoted x_∞. Hence $x_\infty = \lim_{t \to \infty} x_t$.

Continuing, we also obtain from *(17)*

$$\left(\frac{\iota D}{Y}\right)_\infty = a \frac{\iota}{\lambda} \qquad (18)$$

and

$$\left(\frac{\iota D}{Y + \iota D}\right)_\infty = a \left(\frac{\iota}{\lambda + a\iota}\right). \qquad (19)$$

Domar points out that, provided $\lambda > 0$, this last "debt service" ratio—which he identifies as a measure of the debt's burdensomeness—is smaller than 100 percent.

Since it is the tax rate that we are concerned about—will deficits today necessitate incentive-crushing tax rates in the future?—we need to examine the behavior of the tax rate, τ_t. Let us do this.

THE BEHAVIOR OF THE TAX RATE

From *(13)* we have

$$\tau_\infty = \left(\frac{\iota D}{Y + \iota D}\right)_\infty + (\gamma + \beta - a)\left(\frac{Y}{Y + \iota D}\right)_\infty$$

which, upon substitution of *(19)*, yields

$$\tau_\infty = \frac{a(\iota - \lambda) + \lambda(\gamma + \beta)}{\lambda + a\iota}. \tag{20}$$

Now if the tax rate should equal or exceed 100 percent there would be no incentive to work in which case the desired growth path would become infeasible. Even if the limiting tax rate should be less than 100 percent but very large it would be desirable to reconstruct the model to make the targeted growth path a function of work incentives which may in turn be affected by a steep rise of income tax rates. We hope the reader, in the spirit of the Domar model, will settle for an analysis of the following question: on what conditions will the limiting tax rate, τ_∞, be smaller than 100 percent? That is, assuming work incentives are unimpaired by tax rates up to (but not including) 100 percent, on what conditions will the targeted growth path be feasible?

Simple arithmetic shows, assuming $\lambda > 0$, that when $a\iota + \lambda > 0$ then $\tau_\infty < 1$ if and only if $a > \gamma + \beta - 1$. This states that if the proportionate algebraic deficit, a, is greater than $-\lambda/\iota$ then the limiting tax rate will be under 100 percent provided that the algebraic deficit is also greater than $\gamma + \beta - 1$ (which may or may not already be implied by the former inequality). When $a\iota + \lambda < 0$ then $\tau_\infty < 1$ if and only if $a < \gamma + \beta - 1$. This states that if the proportionate *surplus*, $-a$, is greater than λ/ι then the tax rate will be under 100 percent provided that the surplus is greater than $1 - \gamma - \beta$ (which may or may not be implied by the former inequality). Equivalently, there are two "safe" (feasible) zones in which the limiting tax rate is less than 100 percent: one zone in which the algebraic deficit is larger than max $[\gamma + \beta - 1, -\lambda/\iota]$ (which will be a little negative) and another zone in which the algebraic deficit is smaller than $\min [\gamma + \beta - 1, -\lambda/\iota]$—that is, there is a large surplus. The zone between these two is infeasible. A diagram would probably be illuminating but before we can draw it we need to know in what direction τ_∞ changes with changes in a.

Suppose that π (the propensity to consume) were to decrease so that a larger a was required to fulfill the consumption-demand requirement of the targeted income path. While this would certainly call for an initial reduction of the tax rate (to produce the larger deficit) would it also permit a lower limiting tax rate (and hence a permanently smaller tax rate) despite the eventually higher debt service? Taking the derivative of τ_∞ in *(20)* with respect to a we find that, if it exists (implying $\lambda + a\iota \neq 0$), its algebraic sign is the sign of

$$\iota - \lambda - \iota(\gamma + \beta).$$

This expression is negative, and hence an increase of the required a will reduce both the initial and eventual tax rate, if and only if

$$\frac{\iota}{\lambda} (1 - \gamma - \beta) < 1 \quad \text{or} \quad -\frac{\lambda}{\iota} < \gamma + \beta - 1. \quad (\textit{21})$$

Both those readers who believed that an increase of thrift spells an eventual rise of tax rates (since it leads to a higher debt-income ratio) and those readers who believed that it spells a fall of tax rates (since it permits a reduced algebraic surplus and therefore, for a given debt ratio, lower taxes) will be surprised to find that neither result is necessary. Evidently the rise of the debt service ratio will be insufficient to maintain by itself the larger deficit— so that a permanently smaller tax rate will be required (though not as small as in the early years of the larger deficit)—provided the interest rate is not too large.

And now the promised diagram: Figure 8 illustrates our results when $-\lambda/\iota < \gamma + \beta - 1$ and Figure 9 illustrates the case in which $-\lambda/\iota > \gamma + \beta - 1$. The only feature of these diagrams which has not yet been explained can be deduced from *(20)*: As $a \to \pm\infty$, $\tau_\infty \to 1 - \lambda/\iota$ so that τ_∞ is asymptotic to the line $\tau_\infty = 1 - \lambda/\iota$.[2]

---

[2] In discussing *(11)* we showed that a need never be smaller algebraically than $-k$. But this lower limit on the required a does not avert the possibility

FIGURE 8 (top): $-\dfrac{\lambda}{\iota} < \gamma + \beta - 1, \iota < \lambda.$

FIGURE 9 (bottom): $-\dfrac{\lambda}{\iota} > \gamma + \beta - 1, \iota > \lambda.$

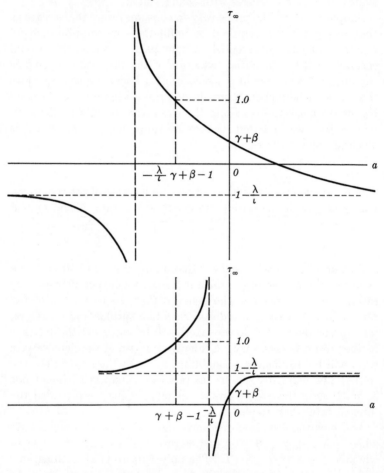

that the required a may fall in the infeasible zone. We assume only that $1 - \gamma - k > 0$, hence $k < 1 - \gamma$ or $-k > \gamma - 1$. Even if $\beta = 0$ this means that the required a could be smaller algebraically than $-(\lambda/\iota)$. And since $\beta > 0$ is possible, a can also be smaller algebraically than $\gamma + \beta - 1$. Therefore nothing precludes the required a from falling in the intermediate infeasible zone of either Figure 8 or 9.

The diagrams describe our results better than words can but let us attempt a brief summary: first, concerning feasibility, should a constant proportionate *deficit* be required to achieve the targeted full-employment income path, the ratio of debt service to taxable income will reach some upper limit, less than 100 percent, rather than increase without limit, as Domar showed. We have demonstrated that, provided $\gamma + \beta < 1$, the same is true of the income tax rate. But should a surplus that is between $1 - \gamma - \beta$ and λ/ι (as a proportion to national income) be required the tax rate will eventually reach 100 percent at which point, presumably, incentives to work will break down and the targeted full-employment growth pattern will cease to be feasible.

Second, concerning the effect of private thrift, should a proportionate deficit be required, an increase of private thrift, by increasing the proportionate deficit required, will raise the limiting ratio of debt service to income, as Domar showed. But despite that rise, the increased deficit will permit a permanently smaller tax rate if the foregoing condition on ι, λ, γ, and β expressed in *(21)* is satisfied. Should a surplus be required, the results are less certain: if the foregoing condition is satisfied and the initially required surplus was sufficiently small that the economy is on the upper curve of Figure 8, then a permanent reduction of tax rates will be possible if the old surplus (hence also the new) is feasible; if the old surplus is not feasible, the increase of thrift may make the (new and smaller) required surplus feasible, and hence prevent the tax rate from reaching 100 percent; but if the new surplus is also infeasible, tax rates can be lower only temporarily as the inevitable approach to a 100 percent tax rate is merely postponed a little. On the other hand, if the old required surplus was so large as to place the economy on the lower curve of Figure 8, then the increase of thrift, by reducing the surplus to a level in the infeasible zone, will eventually cause the tax rate to be positive rather than negative and even to reach 100 percent; but if the reduction of the required surplus is large enough to avoid this zone, the tax rate will escape the latter calamity and merely rise from its initial (possibly negative) value eventually to some higher (possibly positive) limiting value. (A shift from a negative to a positive tax rate is due to the government's move from a creditor position so strong that it must levy negative taxes to a creditor position sufficiently weak that τ_∞, the limiting net tax rate, is positive and possibly very large due to the requirement of a surplus over outlays.)

There are very many cases here so that the following empirical observations may help the reader in deciding which case is the most interesting. In the United States, very roughly:

$\iota = 0.04$ (nominal interest rate on long-term government bonds)

$\lambda = 0.05$ (nominal growth rate, i.e., growth rate of *money* GNP)

$\gamma = 0.20$ (government expenditures as a ratio to GNP)

$\beta = 0.05$ (government noninterest transfers as a ratio to GNP)

so that $(\iota/\lambda)(1 - \gamma - \beta) = 0.60 < 1$. The U.S. is therefore "in" Figure 8. Indeed, even the most "capital-starved" (high ι) and least "publicly needy" (low $\gamma + \beta$) of real-life capitalistic economies surely satisfy this condition. Further since even the most aggressive U.S. growth targets (high λ) are unlikely to require a surplus in excess of 0.75 as a proportion of national income, it seems certain that we are on the upper curve of Figure 8 and safely in the feasible zone!

CONCLUDING REMARKS

We have found that in the Domar model, if initially a deficit was required, an increase of the propensity to save, by increasing the proportionate deficit required to maintain the economy on its targeted full-employment path, will permit a permanently smaller tax rate, despite the concomitant rise of the debt service-income ratio, if the rate of interest on government debt is smaller than the rate of growth of money national income. The necessary and sufficient condition is weaker if the government makes noninterest outlays.

If originally a very large surplus was required to meet the growth target, the increase of thrift, by reducing the required surplus, may so reduce the government's creditor position (hence government interest receipts) that the tax rate will eventually have to be raised above what it would otherwise have been. Indeed, if the new required surplus lies in a critical intermediate zone, the tax rate may reach 100 percent at which point (if not before) the full-employment "growth target"—by which we include the mix between public and private expenditures—will have to be scrapped. On the other hand, the reduction of the required surplus dictated by the increase of thrift may remove the economy from this zone and thereby make possible the targeted growth through a lower tax rate less than 100 percent.

Moral: Private thrift is surely virtuous if it is necessary to the feasibility of the targeted growth path. But if it is not, thrift may yet have a virtue: where the above condition on the rate of interest is satisfied, thrift may be virtuous not because it releases the resources for targeted capital formation—for in this case taxation can do that—but because it permits the growth target to be achieved by lighter taxation than would otherwise be required.

The Golden Rule
of Procreation

- -

It is demonstrated here that there is a "trade-off" between Golden Rule consumption per head and the birth rate or net reproduction rate and that, under certain circumstances, there may exist among possible Golden Rule states—each one corresponding to a certain birth rate—one which is a social optimum. It will be obvious to the reader that this paper does not solve the problem of optimal population growth, just as the Golden Rule of Accumulation does not solve the problem of optimal capital accumulation. Yet this paper may contribute in some small way to a solution of that problem.

THE TRADE-OFF BETWEEN BIRTH RATE
AND GOLDEN RULE CONSUMPTION PER HEAD

For simplicity, we postulate a one-commodity model. We suppose the following concerning the aggregate production function. There is no technical progress. Output is homogeneous of degree one in capital, labor, and land. But land is homogeneous in quality and is unlimited in supply. Hence, if society doubles its capital and labor it can, by spreading its resources over twice the land, contrive to double output. Therefore we may omit land from the production function and make output homogeneous of degree one in capital and labor. We further suppose that both inputs are indispensable to positive output. Marginal productivities are smooth, decreasing, and everywhere positive. Using familiar notation, we may express these conditions as follows:

$$\frac{Q}{L} = F\left(\frac{K}{L}, 1\right) = f(k), \ k = \frac{K}{L}$$

$$F(0, L) = F(K, 0) = 0 \qquad (1)$$

$$F_K(K, L) > 0 \quad F_L(K, L) > 0$$

$$F_{KK}(K, L) < 0 \quad F_{LL}(K, L) < 0.$$

Population and the labor force grow at a constant rate n. This constant will later be made subject to choice. We take population to be a fixed multiple of the labor force for all n; recognition that the higher n, the smaller will be the fraction of the population of working age, would call for a slight modification of the analysis without affecting the results.

$$\frac{\dot{L}}{L} = n, \quad n > 0. \qquad (2)$$

If k is constant then, by virtue of *(1)* and *(2)*, investment per head will be proportional to n:

$$\frac{\dot{K}}{L} = \frac{nK}{L} = nk. \qquad (3)$$

Hence consumption per head, $Q/L - \dot{K}/L$, will be given by

$$c = f(k) - nk. \qquad (4)$$

There is a different golden-age growth path for every k. In one of these growth paths—the Golden Rule (of Accumulation) path—consumption per head is maximal. The existence of a maximum for $n > 0$ is assured by virtue of *(1)* which implies that $\lim_{k \to \infty} f'(k) = 0$. If $f'(0) \geq n$ then there is an interior maximum with respect to k and the maximizing k, say $\hat{k}$, is given by

$$f'(\hat{k}) - n = 0. \qquad (5)$$

If, on the other hand, n is such that $f'(0) < n$ then $f'(k) - n < 0$ for all $k \geq 0$ so that a corner maximum exists:

$$\hat{k} = 0. \qquad (5a)$$

Golden Rule consumption per head is given by

$$\hat{c} = f(\hat{k}) - nk. \qquad (6)$$

Now how does an increase of n affect $\hat{c}$? If the initial n led to a corner or interior maximum at $\hat{k} = 0$ then an increase of n will leave us there; capital, output, investment, and consumption will remain zero. If the initial n led to an interior maximum at some $\hat{k} > 0$ then an increase of n will increase $f'(\hat{k})$; but $f'(k)$ is decreasing in k so $\hat{k}$ will decrease, thus decreasing $f(\hat{k})$, output per head on the Golden Rule path. However, in this case Golden Rule investment per head, $n\hat{k}$, may also decrease. For while n has increased, $\hat{k}$ will decrease, as already explained.

To find the net effect upon $\hat{c}$ of increasing n in this interior case, therefore, we have to differentiate (6) with respect to n and make use of $(5a)$. This yields

$$\frac{d\hat{c}}{dn} = f'(\hat{k}) \frac{d\hat{k}}{dn} - \left(\hat{k} + n \frac{d\hat{k}}{dn} \right)$$

$$= [f'(\hat{k}) - n] \frac{d\hat{k}}{dn} - \hat{k} \qquad (7)$$

$$= -\hat{k} \qquad [\text{by } (5a)].$$

Hence, for all $\hat{k} > 0$, $\hat{c}$ is strictly decreasing in n. But once n is so large that $n = f'(0)$ then $\hat{k} = 0$ and $\hat{c} = 0$; then further increase of n has no effect upon $\hat{k}$ and $\hat{c}$.

Denoting by $\tilde{n}$ the largest value of n for which an interior maximum exists, we may summarize these findings as follows:

$$\hat{c} = c(n), \qquad 0 < n$$
$$\lim_{n \to 0} c(n) > 0$$
$$c'(n) < 0, \qquad 0 < n < \tilde{n} \qquad (8)$$
$$c(n) = 0, \qquad n \geq \tilde{n} > 0.$$

(There is no Golden Rule solution for $n = 0$ because $f'(k)$ is supposed to be positive for all finite k.)

We have shown the connection between the Golden Rule level of consumption per head and the population growth rate. To establish the trade-off between the birth rate and Golden Rule consumption per head we observe that, in a closed economy,

$$n = b - \mu \qquad (9)$$

where b is the "birth rate" (number of births per head) and μ is the "death rate." We take μ as a parameter, not subject to choice. The birth rate is subject to choice.[1]

From *(8)* and *(9)* we obtain the trade-off between b and c:

$$\begin{aligned}
&\hat{c} = h(b), && \mu < b \\
&\lim_{b \to \mu} h(b) > 0 \\
&h'(b) < 0, && \mu < b < \tilde{b} = \mu + \tilde{n} \qquad (10) \\
&h(b) = 0, && b \geq \tilde{b}.
\end{aligned}$$

This trade-off or possibility locus is diagrammed in Figure 10. (Note that there exists a Golden Rule path only for birth rates in excess of the death rate, that is, only for positive rates of population growth.)

THE GOLDEN RULE OF PROCREATION

It is clear that economic satisfaction is a function of consumption. It is equally clear that economic satisfaction is a function of the number of births. It seems likely that, holding per capita consumption constant, parents will prefer more children to less up to a certain point and prefer less children to more beyond that point. (Their neighbors may have different preferences.)

Following the conventional approach, let us suppose that individual utility functions exist, that centralized information about these functions exists, and that there is a "social welfare function" (relating the individual utilities) of such a kind that there exists a "social utility function" which defines "social preferences" over the various possible Golden Rule paths (each one corresponding to a different birth rate).

What information is needed before we can compute and compare the social utilities of these Golden Rule paths? We shall suppose

[1] Actually μ will vary with b if the death rates of various age groups are age dependent. However no great damage is done by taking μ to be invariant to b.

FIGURE 10

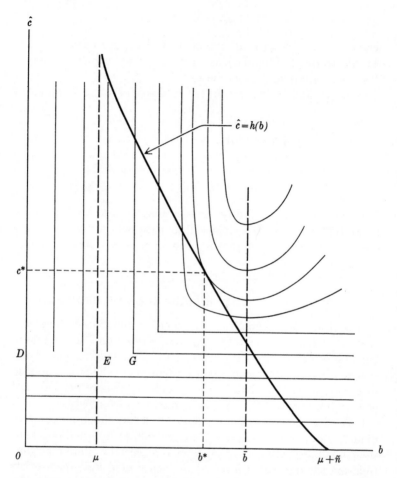

$\hat{c} = h(b)$

that these social utilities can be computed from just two pieces of information: the birth rate and consumption per head. (Both are constants in each Golden Rule path.) It is not unreasonable that social utility should depend upon *per capita* rather than aggregate consumption. Similarly, it is not unreasonable that social utility should be a function of births per parent or the net reproduction rate and therefore upon the birth rate which is a monotonically increasing function of the net reproduction rate.

The next step, of course, is to maximize social utility with respect to the birth rate, subject to the condition $\hat{c} = h(b)$; that is

$$\max_b U(b, h(b)). \qquad (11)$$

If an interior maximum exists it is at that value of b, say b^*, where

$$0 = U_b + U_c h'(b^*) \quad \text{or} \quad -h'(b^*) = \frac{U_b}{U_c}. \qquad (12)$$

The maxim, "choose that steady birth rate which, in a Golden Rule state, will maximize social utility," we may call, for want of a better term, the Golden Rule of Procreation. The result just obtained states that, if an interior maximum exists, then, to satisfy that Rule, one need only equate the marginal cost of the birth rate (in terms of Golden Rule consumption per head) to the marginal social rate of substitution between the birth rate and Golden Rule consumption per head, assuming satisfaction of the second order condition that the stationary value be a maximum.

An interior maximum may not exist. One possibility is that $(U_b/U_c) > -h'(b)$ for all (b, c) on the possibility locus; that is, the social indifference curves cut the possibility locus everywhere from above (as one reads from left to right in a diagram like Figure 10). Then a corner maximum occurs at the biologically maximal birth rate. The same corner maximum may result if the indifference curves are "less convex" than the convex possibility locus. It seems likely however that society would become satiated with births before the biological maximum was approached.

Another possibility is that $(U_b/U_c) < -h'(b)$ for all (b, c) on the downward sloping portion of the possibility locus. In this case there would appear to be a corner maximum at $(\mu, h(\mu))$. But there is no Golden Rule path for $n = 0$ if, as we suppose, $f'(k) > 0$ for all $k > 0$. Hence there is no maximum in this case: for any b close to μ one can always find another b closer to μ which will give more social utility.

The social utility function is constructed from individual (or family) utility functions. But we must recognize that individual utility functions may not exist. This seems especially likely when the choice confronting a family is between consumption and births: as between two states both of which offer "below subsistence" levels of consumption, the family will always prefer that state which gives more consumption regardless of the birth rates associated with the two states. In this case the preferences of the family cannot be represented by a utility function. But it is still possible to represent these preferences by a "preference map." And from such individual preference maps it is presumably possible to construct a "social preference map."

Figure 10 shows such a "social preference map." The diagram is quite similar to one presented by Harvey Wagner.[2] With reference to the family of horizontal lines, any point on a higher line is preferred to any point on a lower line; it is not possible to compensate society for a loss of consumption per head in this region. The quantity of consumption per head $0D$ can be interpreted as the subsistence standard of living. Any point on one of the vertical lines is preferred to any point on a horizontal line. And any point on a more rightward vertical line is preferred to any point on a more leftward vertical line. It should be emphasized that these straight lines are not "indifference curves"; society may not be indifferent between two points on the same straight line. Similarly, the right-angle curves beginning at G need not be interpreted as indifference curves. Farthest from the origin are some ordinary indifference curves that are curvilinear. They show that the community is satiated with births at $\bar{b}$ and that increments in b beyond $\bar{b}$ reduce utility, for fixed $\hat{c}$.

The possibility locus, also shown in Figure 10, has been drawn so as to be tangent to one of the indifference curves. This is the solution described in (12). Another possibility is that the possibility locus goes through a vertex like G; then G is the social optimum among all Golden Rule states. A third possibility is that the possibility locus passes through an endpoint like E; again there is no tangency solution such as described by (12) but E is still the social optimum in this case. But it is also possible, finally, that the locus never rises out of the region of horizontal lines. In this case no social optimum exists.

[2] H. M. Wagner, "The Case for Revealed Preference," *Review of Economic Studies*, Vol. 26 (June 1959), pp. 178–189.

CONCLUDING REMARKS

We have shown that, among all Golden Rule states, there may exist one, corresponding to a certain birth rate, which is socially preferred to all others. Of course society is not constrained to choose only among Golden Rule states. Further, even if it were to restrict itself so, it would wish to take into account the immediate cost of adjusting the historically given capital-labor ratio to the level appropriate to the "optimal" Golden Rule state. Somewhat similarly, it will take a period of time equal to the human life span to get the age distribution of the population in the equilibrium corresponding to the desired birth rate unless the historically given population happened to be in that desired equilibrium. This may also impose costs. Nevertheless it may be conjectured that if the various assumptions of this paper are satisfied—most notably, that land is free and there is no technical progress—then, in the absence of time preference, society would want to choose a path of investment and births which led asymptotically to the "socially optimal" Golden Rule state.

Bibliography on the Golden
Rule of Accumulation
1961-1965

Allais, M., "The Influence of the Capital-Output Ratio on Real National Income," *Econometrica*, Vol. 30 (October 1962), pp. 700–728.

Atsumi, H., "Neoclassical Growth and the Efficient Program of Capital Accumulation," *Review of Economic Studies*, Vol. 32 (April 1965), pp. 127–136.

Beckmann, M. J., "Economic Growth and Wicksell's Cumulative Process," Cowles Foundation Discussion Paper No. 120 (June 1961).

Black, J., "Technical Progress and Optimum Savings," *Review of Economic Studies*, Vol. 29 (June 1962), pp. 238–240.

Cass, D., "Optimum Growth in an Aggregative Model of Capital Accumulation," *Review of Economic Studies*, Vol. 32 (July 1965), pp. 233–240.

———, *Studies in the Theory of Optimal Capital Accumulation*, Doctoral Dissertation, Stanford University, 1965.

Cass, D. and M. E. Yaari, "Individual Saving, Aggregate Capital Accumulation and Economic Growth," Cowles Foundation Discussion Paper No. 198 (December 1965).

Champernowne, D. C., "Some Implications of Golden Age Conditions When Savings Equal Profits," *Review of Economic Studies*, Vol. 29 (June 1962), pp. 235–237.

Desrousseaux, J., "Expansion stable et taux d'intérêt optimal," *Annales de Mines* (November 1961), pp. 31–46.

Diamond, P. A., *Essays in the Theory of Economic Growth*, Doctoral Dissertation, Massachusetts Institute of Technology, 1963.

———, "National Debt in a Neoclassical Growth Model," *American Economic Review*, Vol. 55 (December 1965), pp. 1126–1150.

Fei, J. C. H., "Per Capita Consumption and Growth," *Quarterly Journal of Economics*, Vol. 74 (February 1965), pp. 52–72.

Gale, D., "Optimal Programs for a Multi-Sector Economy with an Infinite Time Horizon," paper presented at the *First World Congress of the Econometric Society*, Rome (September 1965).

Hamada, K., *Economic Growth and Long-Term International Capital Movement*, Doctoral Dissertation, Yale University, 1965.

Howrey, E. P., "Technical Change, Capital Longevity and Economic Growth," *American Economic Review* (May 1965), pp. 397–410.

Inagaki, M., "The Golden Utility Path," Memorandum, Netherlands Economic Institute, Rotterdam (November 1963).

Koopmans, T. C., "On the Concept of Optimal Economic Growth," in *Le Rôle de L'analyse Econometrique dans la Formulation de Plans de Développement*, Vol. 28, Part 1 in the series *Scripta Varia* (Pontificia Academia Scientarium, Vatican City, 1965), pp. 225–287.

Koyck, L. M., and M. J. 't. Hooft-Welvaars, "Economic Growth, Marginal Productivity of Capital and the Rate of Interest," in F. H. Hahn and F. P. R. Brechling, eds., *The Theory of Interest Rates: Proceedings of a Conference Held by the International Economic Association* (New York: St. Martin's Press, 1965), pp. 242–266.

Kurz, M., "Optimal Paths of Capital Accumulation under the Minimum Time Objective," *Econometrica*, Vol. 33 (January 1965), pp. 42–66.

———, "Patterns of Growth and Valuation in a Two Sector Growth Model," *Yale Economic Essays*, Vol. 2 (Fall 1962), pp. 403–474.

Laing, N. F., "A Geometrical Analysis of Some Theorems on Steady Growth," *Journal of Political Economy*, Vol. 72 (October 1964), pp. 476–482.

Levhari, D., "Extensions of Arrow's 'Learning by Doing'," *Review of Economic Studies*, Vol. 33 (April 1966), pp. 117–132.

———, "Further Implications of Arrow's 'Learning by Doing'," *Review of Economic Studies*, Vol. 33 (January 1966), pp. 19–30.

Marty, A. L., "The Neoclassical Theorem," *American Economic Review*, Vol. 54 (December 1964), pp. 1026–1029.

Meade, J. E., "The Effect of Savings on Consumption in a State of Steady Growth," *Review of Economic Studies*, Vol. 29 (June 1962), pp. 227–234.

———, "Life-Cycle Savings, Inheritance, and Economic Growth," *Review of Economic Studies*, Vol. 33 (January 1966), pp. 61–78.

Park, S. Y., *Bounded Substitution, Fixed Proportions and Economic Growth*, Doctoral Dissertation, Yale University, 1965.

Pearce, I. F., "The End of the Golden Age in Solovia: A Further Fable for Growthmen Hoping to be 'One Up' on Oiko," *American Economic Review*, Vol. 52 (December 1962), pp. 1088–1097.

Phelps, E. S., "The End of the Golden Age in Solovia: Comment," *American Economic Review*, Vol. 52 (December 1962), pp. 1097–1099.

———, "The Golden Rule of Accumulation: A Fable for Growthmen," *American Economic Review*, Vol. 51 (September 1961), pp. 638–643.

———, "Second Essay on the Golden Rule of Accumulation," *American Economic Review*, Vol. 55 (September 1965), pp. 793–814.

———, "Substitution, Fixed Proportions, Growth and Distribution," *International Economic Review*, Vol. 4 (September 1963), pp. 265–288.

Radner, R., *Notes on the Theory of Economic Planning*, (Athens: Center of Economic Research, 1963).

———, "Optimal Growth in a Linear-Logarithmic Economy," *International Economic Review*, Vol. 7 (January 1966), pp. 1–33.

Robinson, J., "A Neo-classical Theorem," *Review of Economic Studies*, Vol. 29 (June 1962), pp. 219–226. Reprinted under the title "A Neo-neoclassical Theorem " in J. Robinson, *Essays in The Theory of Economic Growth* (New York: St. Martin's Press, 1962), pp. 120–136.

Samuelson, P. A., "A Catenary Turnpike Theorem Involving Consumption and the Golden Rule," *American Economic Review*, Vol. 55 (June 1965), pp. 486–496.

———, "Symposium on Production Functions and Economic Growth: Comment," *Review of Economic Studies*, Vol. 29 (June 1962), pp. 251–254.

Shell, K., *Patterns of Technical Change and Capital Accumulation*, Doctoral Dissertation, Stanford University, 1965.

Solow, R. M., J. Tobin, C. C. von Weizsäcker, and M. E. Yaari, "Neoclassical Growth with Fixed Factor Proportions," *Review of Economic Studies*, Vol. 33 (April 1966), pp. 79–116.

Solow, R. M., "Symposium on Production Functions and Economic Growth: Comment," *Review of Economic Studies*, Vol. 29 (June 1962), pp. 255–256.

Srinivasan, T. N., "Investment Criteria and Choice of Techniques of Production," *Yale Economic Essays*, Vol. 2 (Spring 1962), pp. 59–116.

———, "Optimal Savings in a Two-Sector Model of Growth," *Econometrica*, Vol. 32 (July 1964), pp. 358–373.

Swan, T. W., "Of Golden Ages and Production Functions," in K. Berrill, ed., *Economic Development with Special Reference to East Asia: Proceedings of a Conference Held by the International Economic Association* (New York: St. Martin's Press, 1964), pp. 3–16.

Tobin, J., "Economic Growth as an Objective of Government Policy," *American Economic Review*, Vol. 54 (May 1964), pp. 1–20.

Uzawa, H., "Optimal Growth in a Two-Sector Model," *Review of Economic Studies*, Vol. 31 (January 1964).

Weizsäcker, C. C. von, "Existence of Optimal Programs of Accumulation for an Infinite Time Horizon," *Review of Economic Studies*, Vol. 32 (April 1965), pp. 85–104.

————, *Wachstum, Zins und Optimale Investitionsquote* (Basel: Kyklos-Verlag, 1962).

Name Index